HOW TO HANDLE
MEDIA INTERVIEWS

D1392121

Andrew Boyd

2000

First edition published 1991

This new edition published 1999 by Management Books 2000 Ltd
Forge House, Limes Road
Kemble, Cirencester
Gloucestershire, GL7 6AD, UK
Tel: 0044 (0) 1285 771441
Fax: 0044 (0) 1285 771055
Email: info@mb2000.com
Web: www.mb2000.com

British Library Cataloguing in Publication Data is available

ISBN 9781852521240

To the truth – and a fairer fight to find it.

CONTENTS

Contents

ACKNOWLEDGEMENTS

Thanks to the following for contributing their gameplans and strategies:

Tony Benn; John Bryant; Andrew Clayton; Philip Ditton; Steve Ellis; Bud Evans; Norman Hart; Liz Howell; Russell Hotten; Jeremy Paxman; John Pike; Alison Sergeant; Des Wilson.

Gratitude also to *The Spectator;* Lynn Barber; Paul Johnson; Sue Arnold; Charles Kennedy and to researcher Tony Williams for his tireless endeavours.

The opinions expressed in this volume will certainly *not* be endorsed by all of the above.

INTRODUCTION

The phone rings: *'Business Daily* calling...'. But *your* business is in trouble and *they* want you for an interview – this morning. What you say could make matters much, much worse, or it could be the turning-point you badly need. Is it worth the risk, or would it be wiser to refuse? But if you say no, will they talk to your rivals instead? And if you agree, what can you say that will help and *how* will you say it?

Whether you are a public relations officer (PRO); politician; spokesperson for a pressure group or in business, you need the media and the media need you, More often than not it may be you who is calling the shots by offering news items to the media; but of all commodities, news is the most unpredictable. Those occasions when a story breaks out and runs wild can seem like mayhem; and right at that moment the last thing you need is exactly what you get – the media hogging your phone lines and hammering at the door. At such times the decision to talk or not to talk can be agonising. In the heat of the moment, you could do with a consultant by your side to help you decide whether the offer is one you really shouldn't refuse; and then to assist you in preparing a response that will move beyond damage limitation towards positive, active promotion. The aim of this book is to do just that.

Good planning is at the heart of every successful strategy – especially in a crisis when the stakes are high. It's important to understand precisely how to plan your message and your delivery if you are to put your point across convincingly under pressure, whilst judiciously dodging the traps. And if your interview is for television, you'll also need to know how to present yourself confidently before the cameras.

The art of media handling is to understand how to match your message to the medium, from delivering a terse 20-second sound-bite for the Nine O'Clock News to negotiating a lubricated lunch with a magazine journalist whilst avoiding handing over ammunition which may be used against you. The skill is to say what they will use in a way that is, hopefully, incapable of distortion.

Well, we can do better than travel hopefully. What follows are strategies for being interviewed on the radio, TV, newspapers and magazines, and advice on promoting yourself in Europe and elsewhere abroad where not only the language but the news agenda are different. To illustrate the message, masters of the craft on either side of the media divide offer their own useful insights and advice.

Comprehensive briefing notes are provided at the back of the book to summarise the information and help you respond rapidly – and wisely – to media opportunities.

The intention has been to go some way towards providing a consultancy within a handbook, offering cool advice when media matters get hot, and a sensible plan of action that will help you turn a threat into a challenge to which you will rise with confidence.

1

HOW TO GRAB THEM BY THE EARS

News is anything that makes a reader say 'Gee Whiz!'
                                                    Arthur McEwen

It screams out from every newspaper and every bulletin – bad news makes good copy. And when journalists flock around, it's more often than not to pick over someone's bones. The problem is that bad news shouts louder than good news. But with the right techniques, even bad news can be turned to your advantage, and if you know *how* to grab them by the ears – and *who* to grab – a ready audience can also be found for your *good* news.

You have a willing and voracious audience. The average UK citizen spends a mind numbing 23 hours a week – that's three working days a week – glued to his TV screen. Most of his news is fed to him from the box, although he and 15 million others supplement their diet of TV dinners with a national newspaper. When the set is eventually allowed to cool down, enough will turn on their radios to support more than 120 local stations. Many more are promised to complement and compete with eight national radio networks. And should the consumer palate still become jaded, there's always the local press, trade press, consumer press, teletext...

Mr Average not withstanding, the audience for your interview will never simply be a faceless mass out there. Bending to your every word will be your constituents; customers; employees; employer; shareholders, and the decision makers you need to influence. And as for Mr Average – never underestimate him – he in his millions forms

3

the authentic voice of public opinion. Not a word will be wasted.

Yet for want of a spark of imagination, media relations are often projected as little more than an exercise in damage limitation. This negative view is damaging in itself. Media relations is about promotion. If you are pro-active, positive, and *promote*, then your good news will be given an airing and even your bad news can be turned to advantage.

Media relations has much in common with marketing. However good your product, if the customers don't know it's available they won't buy. Again, promotion.

Most interviews are the result of a news release. The media has come to you because you first went to them. The first principle is the one that runs throughout this book and is the bread and butter of every business: Give the customers what they want. Why should it be any different with news?

Your campaign plan is simple:

- first determine what you have to offer;
- then find out the needs of the market;
- tailor your product to the market place; and
- promote it hard.

I've Got News For You

> Which do you find more believable... a commercial for a
> product or a documentary programme about it?
>
> Michael Bland[1]

Success in business as in media relations boils down to having the right product and marketing it effectively. News is just another commodity, and the most perishable one there is. But it is tangible enough for people to make their living buying and selling it. It is definable. And whether you are representing a company, a pressure group or a political party, you probably have far more of this commodity at your disposal than you might imagine. But what's it worth?

If by some happy chance you should stumble upon a piece of soft and shiny yellow metal, you would take it to an assayer who will scrutinise it and tell you – hope upon hope – that it is gold. But until it is pronounced gold by the goldman your treasure is worthless. And so it is with news. Information you imagine to be of great value can turn out to be fool's gold. In the end, news is only news if the newsgatherers report it. Which means you need to be familiar with their criteria.

The News Agenda

The newsperson is a broker, buying a commodity to sell into a market place. You have to satisfy him or her, but they have to be able to satisfy their market – the audience. There are markets within markets: international, national, regional, local and special interest. But first we have to settle on the commodity.

> News is the immediate, the important, the things that have impact on our lives.
>
> Freda Morris, NBC[2]

News is whatever is going to affect people. It is about change; imminent or actual. It is about what is happening around me that interests, excites or worries. It follows that news embraces the important and the entertaining. For example, a person living in Hong Kong may be more caught up with the Chinese New Year celebrations than a change of Government in Brazil – unless, that is, that person is a commodity dealer and the commodity in question is coffee.

The hallmark of news is its *relevance*. Whatever the market, the news must be relevant to its audience. It must be about them and impact upon them. The impact of an earthquake is felt most strongly at its epicentre. In the same way, the extent of the impact of a news item will determine the scale of its market as a commodity, and the strength of that impact will determine its position in that market.

Case-Study: News Relevance

Dock workers at Portsmouth container port go on strike over pay and conditions. No further containers are unloaded. The immediate impact is to the port, the dock workers and their families. So the media around Portsmouth mobilises to cover the story. The strike is reported on television, radio and the press; some national business correspondents make a mental note to watch the story and the trade press carries the item.

As the strike continues local coverage looks for new angles: the loss of revenue to the city; congestion in the shipping lanes as container ships stand by, unable to disgorge their cargoes, and then the gradual easing of the logjam as trade is farmed out to other ports. But many containers are already unloaded and unable to be shifted. They are trapped in a no-go area. Gradually, businesses across the country become affected by this strangulation of their supplies.

The business and financial press have had a peck or two, but now begin to gather round. *Business Daily* runs the item, generating wider interest. A smattering of local stories appear in different towns and cities, among them Boston.

A mainframe computer manufacturer in Boston is awaiting the delivery of expensive custom-designed computer motherboards, imported from Japan. With the heart of their computer system stranded in Portsmouth, manufacturing on that line cannot proceed and quickly comes to a standstill. Part of the work force has to be suspended until the parts arrive. The Boston media and the computer press latch on.

It transpires that the Boston plant is producing a much needed new mainframe for the Inland Revenue. The trade press open their columns to the story and a freelance spots it and hawks it to the nationals. Someone asks the inevitable and finds out that, yes, the delay over the computer threatens to stumble the implementation of expected tax cuts in the coming budget. Television swoops on the story and suddenly everyone is running it.

And the Japanese company whose custom-made motherboards are still tied up at the docks has a thing or two to say to the media in *its* country, as do others across the globe whose deliveries have been put on hold and whose shipping has been disrupted.

In this scenario everyone has an interest in bringing this dispute to an end, including those who started it. And the media is a powerful lever. You may be the union leader, the port manager, the director of the plant in Boston, or a city politician. You have a message to put over in the hope of influencing events and an embarrassment of outlets for it – *Willings Press Guide* lists more than 13,000 newspapers and periodicals in the UK alone.

Then there is broadcasting. They are interested in what *you* have to say because they already know about the story, because they have read it or seen it in the media. Media feeds off media. Get a sufficient show of interest from one and the others will often follow.

More often though, the impact of events around you will go unseen and unconsidered by the outside world unless and until you tell them.

Generating News

Like fire, news can be discovered, but it can also be started. The best way to ignite a story is to touch it off against another hot news item. The media is always looking for ways to develop running stories with new angles and reactions.

You may be in a position to bring your expertise and viewpoint to bear on a current issue. Entertainment value lies at the heart of media presentation – even of news. The media loves drama, and the essence of drama is conflict. Newsgatherers will always be interested in controversial issues that affect their audience. They may welcome your reaction to a live issue. But for what you say to be as newsworthy as what you *do*, you will have to convince them you carry personal clout.

Unless you are an acknowledged expert, it will not be enough to represent only yourself. Your voice and your views have to represent a section of opinion and be recognised as such before the media will deal with you. You need to be a spokesperson with a group or a company behind you. In media relations terms, it's the equivalent of a good letterhead. If those are your credentials, then there is nothing stopping you from using them.

Softer Stories

If what you do or what you say impacts upon an audience then it will be newsworthy. And that impact need not always affect them materially. If it stirs an audience emotionally or touches something that interests them, then it may still be news. The appetite for soft news stories is every bit as great as the thirst for the momentous. Most regional television news services cover little enough real news to stretch to a three minute bulletin. How else can they fill the full half hour? A lighter touch is called for.

The *human interest* angle is all around us, but to make a story worthy of media attention it has to be visual and it has to have about it something special. To provide that spin requires the application of style over substance. It's less of what you do, but the *way* that you do it that matters: a construction company pledges one day's profit a month into building a hostel for the homeless and will train and employ jobless teenagers to do the building; a local politician renowned for his loquacity will don a town crier's uniform and bellow through the streets in a sponsored bid to raise cash for a unit for the deaf and dumb; an airline owner makes a bid to cross the Atlantic in a hot air balloon and the result is international publicity. It matters not a whit whether you succeed; if you capture the imagination, you will capture the media. Think in terms of what would make a good picture and you won't go far wrong, and if you can hang your actions to an existing news peg that will help.

Targeting the Media

If the story is five miles out of a local paper's patch, it might as well be a million miles away.

Kim Adams, London Newspaper Group[3]

To target an audience, you will need to focus on:

- audience;
- outlet; and
- contact.

Your audience will be defined by the relevance of your message within a given locality or interest group.

8

Ask yourself:

- who does it *affect*?
- who will be *interested*?
- who will feel the *impact*?

Your outlet will supply news to one of the five categories already described:

- international;
- national;
- regional;
- local; and
- special interest.

Serving the market under one or more of those headings will be:

- broadcasting:
  - TV: satellite or cable?
  - radio;
- newspapers;
- trade press;
- magazines;
- electronic information (teletext and Prestel); and
- press agencies and freelances.

You will need to follow each branch until you get to the fruit. After precisely targeting your outlets you will need to precisely target specific named contacts within them and introduce yourself.

Like getting along in all things, media relations is a matter of who you know. The advantages of employing a PR specialist is that he or she does the cultivating for you. If you intend to do it yourself, you will still need some assistance. Media directories can supply. Some useful titles serving the UK are given in Appendix 11.

The profile of your audience is as important in media relations as it is in advertising. Who do you *want* to hear your news? If you are a businessman concerned with reaching like-minded professionals, then the trade press or a business programme would be an obvious target. If you are a politician seeking re-election, then it must be the local media. If you are campaigning for new legislation to help the homeless, then a combination of national and urban targeting is needed.

Beware of simply playing to your preferences and leaving it to your hunches. Your personal tastes and interests are unlikely to be representative. Take viewing habits: a national survey found that most UK businesspeople seem to be too busy to be bothered with TV – that is, compared to the average person. The typical business person found the time to chalk up *only* 13 hours of viewing a week[4]. Take education: the typical citizen in the UK, aged between 16 and 69, has absolutely *no* educational qualifications, according to the OPCS General Household Survey[5]. Fortunately, present school-leavers fare somewhat better, but most still fall short of 'A' level standard.

The fact that you have a professional interest in this volume means you are unlikely to be a regular reader of Britain's most widely bought newspapers, the *News of the World* and *The Sun*. Yet each of these attracts twice as many readers as the quality papers combined sold on the same day. Fifteen times as many people take *The Sun* as read the *Financial Times*, whose national circulation figures are comparable only to those of the decidedly different *Morning Star*.

If your strike rate is to be high, your message will have to be adapted to these different markets. Audience profiles are available for broadcasting as well as the press. With them you will be able to target your news message effectively and to overturn any false assumptions:

> Sky news appeals to two lots of people at once: opinion formers and lower middle and working class people. The appeal is to the factory floor and the boardroom in one go.
>
> Liz Howell, Managing Editor, *Sky News*

Once you have identified the key publications and programmes that could call you for interview, familiarise yourself with them so they cease to be an unknown quantity. This will help you adapt your message to suit.

Adapting Your Message to the Market

Adaptation is largely a case of looking, listening and imitating what you see. You will need to uncover the media agenda, and tailor what you produce to suit. Coming chapters explain how to put yourself in their shoes and match your needs to their wants. And these can differ dramatically. Contrast the following, from *The European* and *The Birmingham Post*:

> Within a European dimension, certain things dictate the agenda: monetary union is one; big business deals and huge marketing exercises which cross borders are others. With the single market there are stories which affect the whole of Europe. What we're trying to do is to produce news, views and comment which will have real meaning for the lives of businessmen, whether they work in Frankfurt, Madrid or Helsinki. There's a big common pool of people who need to know what's going on.
>
> John Bryant, Editor, *The European*

> We've got a high concentration of large companies based in the heart of industrial England, but the nationals don't tend to cover them in depth, especially subsidiaries and their activities. So our role is to inform our readers what's happening locally.
>
> Russell Hotten, Business Editor, *The Birmingham Post*

Clued-up businesspeople will find an opportunity for promotion in either publication for news items. But, as we know, the media's idea of what makes a good story is often the kind of stuff you or I might prefer to hush up. Russell Hotten continues:

> The editorial criteria are, I suppose, something that's going to give the reader a bit of a buzz, a little bit of a shock, maybe excite them; a good juicy story. In terms of business that's a big takeover; a boardroom row; somebody being sacked, major job losses or major job gains; something of that sort.

So news promotion has a dual aspect. There are times when it has to involve damage limitation. On such occasions media expertise becomes crucial, because cover-ups simply don't work. If a story is big enough and bad enough it will 'holler from the roof tops' however hard you try to hush it up. But even bad news can be turned to your positive advantage, as we will see later.

Delivering Your Message

How you get your news message to the market is as crucial as how a company delivers its products. The four main ways are the:

- news conference;
- news briefing;
- news release; and
- personal contact.

Now turn those on their head. *All* are about personal contact. The news conference and the news briefing are ways of talking to the media under controlled conditions – supposedly – and the news release is, in effect, a begging letter saying, 'please ring me.' Why wait for them? Better still: fax and phone. Do both.

The News Conference

> A candidate shows up for a press conference. There aren't three people who are going to speak to him. There are 60 reporters there. They are sticking their microphones in his face. People pushing, people shoving. Even an experienced candidate can get ruffled.
>
> *The Media Show*[6]

Let's dispense with news conferences and press briefings first. The conference is a full-blown set-piece affair to launch a product or a campaign or make some important announcement. *Don't bother* – unless what you have to say is so important that you simply can't do it justice in a news release, or you would have to give interviews to so many reporters that it would be impossible to get round them individually or in small groups at a series of less formal press briefings. If you simply must make a grand entrance let an expert arrange it for you. To avoid fouling too many print deadlines set a date early in the month, before midweek and arrange to finish by noon with the option of lunch afterwards.

The press conference belongs to an antediluvian era where deadlines meant the closing time at the bar. The crush of journalists and pressure of modern deadlines (hourly in radio, constant in 24 hour satellite news) can mean everyone having to push their different angles at once, asking divergent questions simultaneously, with such determination to cut in that you seldom have time to complete one point before someone in the pack drags you in a different direction. Fine only for the infantry in the trade press and the weeklies who can bide their time until the airborne brigade buzzes off.

As far as the electronic media is concerned, press conferences are best left to the press and the President. They are a long-winded way of getting a 20 second comment and an almost impossible vessel for providing two minutes' worth of useable material for a longer report.

If the story is worth covering, the electronic media will always want to interview you *on your own* – TV so it can light you correctly and radio so the reporters can get their microphones to you. And both so they can get the answers they want rather than have to make do with the statements you give. Furthermore, radio and TV project an intimacy that is best achieved away from the formality of the podium.

Broadcasters should be given the chance to interview you *first*, on the strict understanding that nothing will be transmitted until after the conference has begun; failing that, give them clear access to you immediately afterwards, at an appointed time. There can be better ways to establish rapport and get your message across to the media.

News Briefings and Facility Visits

A simpler, less formal, and in many ways more satisfying way all round of getting background information across to the media is to call a news briefing. Target a few key contacts from different media outlets to join you over a light lunch. Then you can talk. With the choicest of contacts you can give your message to more of the world than you might at first imagine. And you can always stage a similar exercise over breakfast.

If your aim is to introduce yourself and your company to the media or strengthen relations, then you could consider a facility visit. This is not a glib option. Your guided tour and succinct briefing will require careful planning and the co-operation of your staff in carrying out escort duties and offering explanations, food and *largesse* to the assembled multitude.

The visit should be timed to coincide with a news announcement, so you have something more to offer than tea and biscuits. Interview and photo-opportunities will have to be laid on, and a press room provided with phone, fax and other facilities.

The News Release

This is usually the prime point of contact with the media. Despite their pivotal role, the overwhelming majority of news releases are unspeakable garbage and as such are customarily binned. As a news editor on a local radio station I had to sift each morning through a weighty pile of up to 80 of these environmentally unfriendly tree-killers. As I also had to prepare bulletins and organise the day's news coverage simultaneously, I would arrange for the newsroom secretary to remove the offending articles from their envelopes to give me the edge. That meant I could devote a full five seconds to each:

- Lavish propaganda sheet from Colonel Ghaddafi – bin.
- Missive from the Israeli embassy... Come on, this is *local* radio – bin.
- Technical spec. on an in-flight refuelling system – at least, that's what I *think* it is – with photograph – bin... Wait, it's from a local company. What do they want us to do, describe the picture to our listeners? Any new jobs? Anything in it at all? No... Bin.
- Novosti says some Russian has ridden his motorbike up a mountain and left it there as a monument to Soviet engineering. Doesn't say how he got back down, though... bin.
- Ah. 'Newtown Hypermarket creates 300 jobs.' That's worth looking at...

Some news releases fail because they are telling the right story to the wrong people; others because they are telling it the wrong way. The rest of the rejects simply don't have a story to tell. When there is one, the angle – the 'what's in it for me,' i.e. what impacts on the audience – has to be right there in the headline or it will be overlooked by busy editors. That is guaranteed.

If you want to sell something to an editor, you will need to offer him/her something they will buy. And to do that you may have to tailor the same message to suit several different outlets with the angle for each individual audience in bold at the top. Highlight the local angle and the local impact for the local media. Save the technical details for the trade press. Keep it factual and newsy for the quality papers, and push the 'gee whiz!' and human interest angles to the tabloids and consumer magazines. It's what wordprocessors were made for.

Post news releases if they are *certain* to arrive at least five working days in hand; fax them if the story is imminent. And if it's urgent, ring the media to alert them that your fax is on the way. Better to be a face or a voice than a postmark.

> I would expect big companies to have contacts on a newspaper that they would use at a personal level, and not to just rely on press releases.
>
> John Bryant, Editor, *The European*

Pictures

> The trouble with most handout pictures that come with press releases is that they look like prison or passport photos.
>
> John Bryant

Pictures need to be lively, interesting and attention-grabbing. Few are. 'People within companies are too self-conscious about the sort of pictures they send out,' continues John Bryant. 'You either get the head and shoulders or the man behind a beautifully composed desk. They look static – unreal.'

He offers the following advice: 'Get your photographer, or hire one for the day, and let him wander round and shoot what *really* goes on in a company – people at work, doing things or taking meetings. You'd get what any newspaper would be trying to produce, a real insight into what happens. And you can edit them before they go out.' (For more on pictures see Chapter 6.)

Deadlines

> Journalists often move in packs and brandish notepads and tape recorders. Their plea of the deadline never fails as a verbal laxative.
>
> Sarah Dickinson[7]

You may have the right story and the right contact, but the wrong time... Be mindful of media deadlines and work with them. Regard them as a window of opportunity, and get in there while it's open.

- Radio news coverage is usually set up in the morning by the News Editor. Deadlines are hourly so reporters are always in a hurry. Breakfast shows are planned by a producer the previous day.
- Regional TV plans its evening news programme in the morning.
- Some items will already be in the cans. There will be bulletins throughout the day. An editor, news editor and producers will plan the coverage.
- National TV news will produce programmes and bulletins throughout the day, each with its own producer. Allow as much lead time as possible.
- National daily newspapers will have tomorrow wrapped up by 16.30 today.
- For Sunday newspapers, the week begins on Tuesday.
- Regional evening newspapers would prefer to hear from you by first post, but a call before midday might just scrape in.
- A weekly newspaper will go to press the day before it hits the streets. So its last news items will need to be in the day before that. To be safe give them three days' grace.
- Magazines and supplements can have outrageously long lead times. As a freelance I have had to produce current affairs analysis for a bi-monthly *eight weeks* before it went to press. I

16

still take a certain satisfaction in anticipating the collapse of the Berlin Wall by a fortnight. Check with the magazine and consider how your copy will wear several months on. What you would say then may differ from what you would say now.

All said, the news media likes nothing better than a burst of adrenalin to take it up to the deadline – providing the story is worth it – as can be seen from this example from Channel 4's *Business Daily*:

> In the early morning we can finish an interview in the City at 8 o'clock and get it on air by 8.25. There's no problem with that, but it means we've got to be on the spot at around 7.45 when the crew are in overtime.
>
> For our main programme, which is the lunchtime one at 12.30, we can be doing something in the City at 12.10, but obviously we're reluctant to do that too often, because we don't like stuff being scrambled on air.
>
> By and large, we like to schedule interviews reasonably early in the morning, so we can consider what the person is saying carefully.
>
> If the story's important we can reschedule it right up to the last minute, but we work out our crew schedule – where they go; how long it's going to take for them to get from one place to another – at about 6 o'clock the evening before.
>
> Andrew Clayton, Editor *Business Daily*, Channel 4

A cautionary note: however well you may have targeted, prepared and delivered your missive, the news agenda is constantly changing as breaking stories jockey for prominence. Your expansion plans, sit down protest or resounding assault on your political opponent, which might have led yesterday's news, could well be squeezed out altogether by war, famine or flood. Keep trying and hope for a slow news day.

On a more positive note, if it will keep, consider waiting for a slow news day and make your play. Most days in July and August; the morning after a bank holiday and Monday mornings are a reasonable bet.

Embargoes

Think again. When you are asking a journalist to embargo a story, you are asking him not to use the very tools of his trade.

Dina Ross[8]

There may be times when you would welcome some publicity – but not just yet. You might be at the final stages of a company takeover; or at the point of announcing a major construction project just as soon as the last papers are signed.

Embargoes are a useful way of attempting to regulate the flow of sensitive information, like the findings of a report or an inquiry; announcements such as the New Year's Honours List, or anything that would cause embarrassment or be detrimental if it were publically leaked beforehand. The embargo is the crucial date and time before which your story cannot be published or broadcast – you hope.

NEW REPORT SAYS HOMELESSNESS IS AT AN ALL-
TIME HIGH
GOVERNMENT ACTION 'TOO LITILE TOO LATE'

EMBARGO: NOT TO BE RELEASED UNTIL 12 NOON
SEPT.19

Make sure the word EMBARGO looms large at the top of the news release and can't be overlooked; intentionally or otherwise.

You will need to choose your embargo time wisely to suit the publication deadlines of your target media. If the local evening newspaper hits the streets at 14.00, the pressure to break an embargo time of 15.00 would be temptation beyond endurance. But make doubly sure that having settled on a sensible time, you make no concessions to a soul. If the media suspects an embargo is being broken they'll rush like lemmings to publish, and there will be nothing you can do apart from taking the huff and threatening to hold your breath until you turn blue. Embargoes are not legally binding, and if you offend the media you'll miss them more than they will miss you.

Make it clear that all *interviews* arising from your news release are also subject to embargo, and spell that out *before* somebody comes out to record you. They should already have figured on that, but however large you have written the word embargo, don't assume they've noticed it. Then when you have completed the recording, check again that they will stick to the embargo.

> There have been occasions when we have been given tip-offs the night before that something is happening. Obviously, we're never told precisely *what*, but we're told a major company is 'doing something important... can you make your crew available at such a time...' and we've done that.
>
> Andrew Clayton, *Business Daily*

Embargoes are not greatly liked by the media, but they have their uses. It allows them to get a good story in the cans ready to go the moment the embargo is lifted. From your point of view, they allow you to get the major interviews over and done with before the rush sets in. But it needs to be a good story for the media to want to be bothered with it.

Where embargoes fail is in trying to contain a major running story. If the hounds are already onto the scent they will ignore your protests or get what they want from another source. Sooner or later the story will break, however you try to contain it. It could be sooner than you intended.

Building up Contacts

> A good contacts book is the most treasured possession of any reporter or researcher... even more treasured, I often suspect, than our cuttings books. We massage our egos as we read those yellowing cuttings. But our contacts book is the most essential tool of our trade.
>
> Harold Evans[9]

The reporter's hallowed contacts book contains the names of those who offer him his livelihood; the people whose comments inform and enliven his copy. If you have something to say, it's in their interest to have your name in their book, and for you to have their name in yours.

So, why wait for them to come to you? Media relations are about precisely that, establishing personal contact with individual reporters in the news media to whom you can offer your stories. The contacts to go for are the specialists covering your particular field, such as business, industrial or political correspondents. You will also need the decision-makers, who determine what is to be covered. In broadcasting terms you want the editors, news editors, producers, programme organisers and programme controllers. Get to know them by name and, having made personal contact, ask for their home telephone numbers as well. The more ambitious among them will regard themselves as on duty 24 hours a day and may be willing to oblige.

In television, don't neglect the researchers. Often these are the people who will come up with the ideas that make a programme work. They're the footsloggers and unsung heroes of TV, who will often carry out the interviews themselves anyway.

Make contact with a reputable news agency. If your story is up to it they will make it their business to flog it around as many outlets as possible. On a UK national basis, the respected Press Association service is taken by most of the media.

If you are targeting two outlets under the same roof, do so twice. Don't rely on *anyone* to pass *anything* on. Contacts need to be cultivated. It can be a good idea to throw a buffet meal once a year for local media representatives and any other specialists that you are dealing with regularly or would like to deal with more often. Avoid Christmas, as whoever is still standing by the time it comes round to your bash would probably rather they were doing something more sensible, such as their Christmas shopping.

Having built up your list of contacts, you will need to maintain it. There is a high turnover of personnel in the media.

Masterclass

Throughout the course of the *Today* programme more than five million listeners tune in for 20 minutes or more. Car and Northern Europe listeners push their reach up to seven million each morning.

Daily Express [10]

20

Bud Evans, an Editor of the Today programme, BBC Radio 4

You need to understand the kinds of stories that are going to make. And the kinds of stories that are *not* going to make are from the endless handouts and press releases from manufacturers' press officers who only do it to keep up their strike rate. Most of this stuff doesn't get *anywhere* apart from the trade press. This is not the way to get at the consumers – the buyers.

The way to do it is to respond to the kind of stories that are *already* about. For example, every Christmas there is a scare about foreign toys coming into the country that are dangerous because they don't meet the kinds of standards we set our own manufacturers. We would need a British toy manufacturer to talk about the risks and the way UK companies overcome them to produce safer products. They stand a better chance if they know what the news is, and understand how they can respond to it.

SO YOU ADVISE THEM TO RESPOND TO NEWS THAT IS CURRENT?

That will have the highest strike rate, certainly. There are people who work for commercial companies who make themselves experts on a subject and we go to them, recognising that they are part of a company and giving their name on occasions.

Rentokil has made itself an expert on a variety of matters from woodworm and damp in the home to hazardous chemicals. It offers itself for interviews when a related story breaks. Sometimes the company succeeds. It does it by the phone or fax, not so much press releases, because they are responding to a story that day.

WHAT'S THE BEST WAY OF LETTING THE MEDIA KNOW YOUR STORY?

If it's a press release, it has to tempt us in the first paragraph. They have to find some angle that is going to make it newsworthy. The number of press releases we get into the

Today office! A lot of them don't go beyond first glance, because it's going to be a manufacturer's name on the top, and why should *Today* be interested in a new product?

Broadcasters are sceptical about plugs for products and quite rightly too! They are more likely to get a mention if they stress the newness of the *technique used* than the finished product. Otherwise a new product will appeal only to the trade.

I'm all in favour of people making individual contacts then following up with a press release and following up again with a phone call. With a fax it's much easier. People can fax into the middle of night to us, and do.

It's important to get yourself on in the early morning when the audience is greater than the rest of the day put together. It's so important that company offices are staying open longer. Press officers are available at home. They give their chief executive's number. They're expected to get up early in the morning, and it's in their interests to do so, to make themselves available and realise that the most important thing they can do in that segment of the day is address themselves to the media.

John Bryant, Editor, The European

It's no good dressing up something that's not there, and I think a lot of companies cry wolf too often. They send out press releases that actually contain no news, and editors get to know which companies devalue the coinage.

John Pike, Manager Media Affairs, Shell UK

Shell has a happy tradition of not crying wolf. We don't send out press releases every time the Chairman makes a statement to staff, or we open a new service station. A press release probably has about five seconds to make an impact. I believe the currency of the Shell press release is still such that probably the reader will look at it for *eight* seconds instead of five.

We don't play gimmicks with the press and the media. We don't have hoards of bimbos phoning around, saying 'I sent you a press release, when are you going to use it?' We don't put ourselves around unless we have something important to say, and then when we do, the chances of us being then invited along to the *Today* programme, *PM* or the *Money Programme*, are much higher.

Philip Ditton, Chief Information Officer and Deputy Director of Public Relations, CBI

If you've got a genuine story to tell, you shouldn't have any difficulty interesting the media in it, given a basic understanding of how to approach journalists. But you've got to have some straw to make those bricks. Question number one is what is your target audience? Who are you aiming at? You've also got to exercise good timing and judgement. It's no use pushing stuff out late in the day, because you'll miss press deadlines. Get the copy in early, but not too early. Follow it up with a call for target journalists, telling them something's coming; what it's all about, where they can get back to you – and where they can get you after hours as well.

Alison Sergeant, News Editor, BBC Radio Cambridgeshire

Corporate PR people are very foolish to overlook local radio, because in practice more people are listening to local radio than listen jointly to many of the network radio stations. Local radio is a very hungry beast with many, many hours of airtime to fill every day. Therefore it is hugely easy to sell a story to local radio.

If you can identify *who* is listening to *what* at what time of the day, you can very sensibly target where you want to get your message across. Your local radio station might have a business slot, so you can get your message to the local business community.

If you want to go for mass appeal, most people are listening during the breakfast time hours of between seven and nine. Listen to the programme, find out the sort of stories they are covering and how they cover them.

We can communicate stories of interest to a wide audience, particularly useful if there are large numbers of employees involved. There's nothing more massaging than to hear something about your company on the air.

If it's an urgent story that's happening today: you've just landed a two and a half million pound contract, you'd be stupid not to tell us straight away. Send us a fax or phone us, or phone us and send us a fax. We'll use the story instantly.

HOW OFTEN DO COMPANIES OVERLOOK THEIR OWN STORIES?

They overlook a tremendous amount. There are endless stories you discover when you meet businessmen at lunches, such as Rotary. Once you fall into conversation they tell you about all sorts of developments they wouldn't bother to contact you about. I wish to goodness people would release that information to us and let us know, without me having to fight for it!

I can only assume people don't know what *is* a good story, or what is a *story*, full stop. I wish they would sometimes step back from what they are doing and think, 'Hey, could this be of interest?' It might not be a product. It could be the way they handle things; the little things that might change people's lives to a greater or lesser degree for the better,

Liz Howell, Managing Editor, Sky News

Sky News broadcasts to an unusual cross-section of people. It is played constantly in offices in Whitehall; most of the main newspaper editors have *Sky News* on, and our competitors, the BBC and ITV, have it on all the time. You've got a huge cache of opinion formers. So you can speak to the chairmen of other companies or make use of the fact that we've also got a committed audience of lower middle and working class people.

For example, when there was a potential strike on the BP oil rigs. we were the only television that the rigs could get. So we had an interesting dialogue with the company, which at first wouldn't talk to us, and then wanted to talk to us all the time, because they realised it was the main way of getting through to their workforce.

Russell Hotten, Business Editor, The Birmingham Post

Of course, sometimes people unknowingly break embargoes... Rover group won an important award from the Design Council for one of their engines. An embargoed press release was allegedly sent out to all the media. It didn't arrive at *The Birmingham Post* and we knew nothing about it.

We actually got a tip-off, four days before the story, from another source. So we ran the story. The Design Council claimed we broke the embargo...

If somebody sends us an embargoed press release, it's still possible that the story could leak out through other sources. If the story concerns a contract abroad and it is running in newspapers in that country and Reuters pick it up there and send it over, what do you do? You can't hang on to the embargo because the story has become public knowledge.

2

SHOULD YOU GIVE THE INTERVIEW?

The answer to the question, *should I appear on this*, is 99 times out of 100, 'Yes you should!' Because you are going to have an opportunity of saying something which will be denied you if you say 'no comment.' Other people will say things to your detriment, but you can cover that ground and make something positive even out of a negative-sounding story.

Bud Evans

Sound advice. But let's put in an immediate rider: *never* be pressurised into giving an interview. Most publicity can be turned into good publicity, but there are exceptions... Before you agree to stick your neck on the block you must be certain it would be in the best interests of your company or organisation and yourself. You will need to know whether what the programme makers want to hear matches what you are prepared to say – in other words, will the airtime be to your advantage?

To work that out you'll need to know:

- the subject of the interview;
- the format of the interview; and
- the line of questioning.

The type of programme or publication will give you a good clue. If it's one of those hard-hitting consumer watchdog programmes or a heavyweight current affairs show, brace yourself! If it's local radio, press or regional TV, then breathe a little easier. These tend to be softer focused and have more time for good news stories to cheer the folks at home.

If you're nervous or inexperienced the temptation will be to cut and run. The line of least resistance will be to take the safe solution and turn down the interview. But to do so could be to miss a gift of invaluable peak-time publicity.

Jeremy Paxman from *Newsnight* puts forward two good reasons for agreeing to be interviewed – the carrot and the stick: 'First you've got something you want to sell; a position or a product. Secondly, in not doing so it can seem as if you've got something to hide.' That view is pervasive:

> In my experience, that generally is the case, that if they don't talk they *do* have something to hide.
>
> Always talk to us, either on or off the record, but never ignore us.
>
> Russell Hotten, *The Birmingham Post*

Reasons for Refusing

Fear of the unknown is the worst of all reasons for refusing to give an interview. Here are some others that are almost as specious...

- Television is always on the attack...
- You always concentrate on the negative...
- You're only around when things go wrong, you never call us
- when things are going well...
- The timing is all wrong   if we give an interview now it
- might damage our negotiations...
- We never discuss company policy on TV – it's bad business...
- My diary was booked solid three months ago – how can you call us up at the last minute and expect us to drop everything...
- There are conflicts of style. Television is too pushy. You like to argue, we prefer to discuss...
- How can you expect to cover an issue as complicated as this in just two minutes?
- We don't believe in washing our dirty linen in public...

- Confidence is everything in business... one statement out of place could wipe thousands off our share value...

That's what people often *say*... but what they usually *mean* is this:

- You've caught me by surprise...
- I don't want to be made to look a fool...
- I'm not sure our case is strong enough to stand up in public...
- TV scares me rigid...
- I'm too inflexible to grab an opportunity when one is staring me in the face...

It's not hard to find an excuse for refusing an interview when you're inexperienced. But the reasons for *agreeing* to be interviewed are far more compelling. You will:

- raise your organisation's profile;
- promote the interests of your cause;
- enhance your company's image;
- gain valuable free publicity;
- perhaps get your organisation out of a tight corner; and
- boost your own career prospects.

> Get the game rules sorted out, but remember, the nature of television is that it's their ball park; it's their ball; it's their game.
>
> John Pike, Shell UK

Potential interviewees tend to go down with journophobia when they don't know the rules of the game or when they've played the game before and lost. But instead of backing off, what you need is to understand the rules and be taught how to play to win. Then the threat becomes a challenge and almost any request for an interview can become an opportunity that's too good to miss. And it's not as difficult as it may sound. Put it another way – when was the last time you heard of a politician turning down an interview?

> If you have the opportunity of influencing people you take it. That is the reason I do interviews. I see the House of

28

2. Should You Give the Interview

Commons now as a sort of television programme to which you are elected.

Last year I did 323 radio broadcasts and 171 television. Clearly, if you tot up the six million for Question Time and perhaps 50,000 for a local radio station, you are having an input into public understanding.

During the Gulf War I had five or ten [interviews] a day sometimes, and undoubtedly it had an influence. I had 12-13,000 letters, many triggered off by what they heard me say on radio, which is far more than would ever have read a speech in Hansard.

Tony Benn, Labour MP for Chesterfield

I attach very great importance to the press and broadcasting, which are the main means by which we get our message across.

Peter Mandelson, former Labour Party Campaigns and
Communications Director[1]

Many businesspeople, however, are uneasy about being interviewed because they suspect a conflict of interests. Corporate bodies tend to be conservative and cautious. Business is built on careful planning and confidence, but it is established by the cut and thrust of entrepreneurs who spy the main chance and seize it.

News is pretty much the same. Stories break and opportunities present themselves. Journalists chase leads and convert them into copy. The rush is on to clinch the story before the opposition get to it. Looked at this way, the worlds of journalism and business are not so far apart.

Another excuse for turning down free publicity is that news can break at the most inconvenient moments – because those inconvenient moments themselves are often newsworthy: a fire destroys a warehouse; your party slips in the opinion polls; your company loses a major order.

It's a difficult time for you and the unexpected makes the pressures even greater than normal. The last thing you need is the media turning their spotlight onto your problem. News is about change – actions that are out of the ordinary; events that are often upsetting and disturbing. And while you're still reeling, the reporters catch wind of it and descend on you like vultures. Or that's the way it can seem.

29

The answer is to deal with it as you would any difficulty in business. Be prepared for it, set up a mechanism in advance to deal with the media in a crisis, be positive, and be ready to turn a setback into a springboard.

Look at it like this: your warehouse might have burnt down, but you'll get that back on the insurance anyway. It's given you a first-rate opportunity for thousands of pounds' worth of free publicity, which, with the right know-how, you can easily turn to your advantage.

What is important to your preparation is that you know the angle that the interviewer intends to take. The news angle means the facet of the story they are focusing in on and their reasons for so doing. Will their perspective be critical of you, or supportive?

At the very least you can use it for damage limitation – by taking the opportunity to apologise that supplies will be disrupted and give an assurance that you are doing everything possible to put matters right. The message that will come over is of a caring company which is more concerned about the plight of others than the inconvenience to itself. All to your credit. But the stakes can be far higher and playing the media game can get you out of serious trouble. Let's take some actual examples.

The oil industry has been investigated several times under suspicion of making a killing at the consumer's expense. For most people, their only contact with the oil firms is at the garage forecourt, where they are usually grumbling over petrol prices.

In 1990 the industry was exonerated by the Monopolies and Mergers Commission. Their chief criticism, after pouring over mountains of paperwork, was that the industry had failed to explain its business to the public. How many people realise that in real terms petrol is the cheapest it has ever been, and sixty per cent of the price of a gallon goes straight to the Government in tax?[2]

But if the Monopolies and Mergers Commission finding had swung the other way, John Pike of Shell UK warns the consequences could have been dire:

> Goodness knows what might have happened. We might have been broken down into smaller units. Our whole business might have been totally disrupted. It could have cost us millions in the long run, by being forced to sell off sites.

30

If people don't understand you, there is more chance that they're not going to believe you. If they understand the mechanism of petrol prices, there's a much better chance they will accept price rises.

And it's not just the public you can influence through TV, radio and the press – the media offers you access into the very homes of the people who wield the power and have your destiny in their hands: 'Through the medium of television, you can explain to the shareholders, politicians and people on these committees what your business is about,' says John Pike, '*It can affect your very existence.*'

An oil spill in the River Mersey landed Shell with a million pound fine. Hard to imagine how that could be turned into a public relations exercise. Yet when the media picked up on river pollution again Shell grabbed the opportunity, as John Pike explains: 'Shell was able to say what it was doing to ensure that this sort of thing can't happen again. To have this chance to explain oneself on prime time television... I know no better way of communicating.'

When traces of salmonella were found to be statistically linked to Farley's plant at Kendal, Cumbria, the whole range of baby milks was withdrawn and the plant shut down. The Farley spokesmen showed such concern, such a readiness to be open with the general public, such frankness with the press, that the crisis soon blew over and Farley's regained its market share within 18 months.

Dina Ross[3]

These are all chances that could have been lost, if the companies concerned had taken the easy way out, 'played safe' and said 'No.' And remember, there is nothing to stop your rivals from saying 'Yes' and making capital out of your misfortune. That said, there may be occasions when it would be inappropriate or downright damaging to go in all guns blazing.

In a labour relations situation, rule number one is don't negotiate through the media.

31

Logistics also come into it. There will be days when it will be physically impossible to field a spokesman. Companies don't exist for the media, as some journalists seem to think.

That said, it's important to retain the initiative. The prudent company will seek to anticipate events and have someone available at crucial times.

Philip Ditton, CBI

Pre-interview Checklist

In general a contributor is entitled to be informed in advance about the general area of questioning. In exceptional circumstances – for example, programmes investigating practices which are against the public interest – programme makers may need to be secretive about their intentions.

This does not absolve journalists from the obligation to ensure that all broadcast material is fair, just and true.

BBC Guidelines for Factual Programmes

In the world of TV and radio news you can never be sure quite who will approach you to ask for an interview. From the blizzard of different programmes a bewildering array of different people could contact you – usually by phone and always in a hurry. The caller could be a researcher for a current affairs programme, a news editor for an evening regional TV show, or the reporter who will actually conduct the interview.

Irrespective of title, the caller will be acting on a brief drawn up by the programme producer, who has decided which items are wanted for the programme, and how they should be covered. The producer will have a story in mind and commission a reporter to gather the facts that will make that story stand up. He will be searching for an interviewee with a viewpoint which matches the angle he intends to take, and will have come to you for that purpose. If you think that sounds like news management, you'd be correct. An open-minded quest for the truth seldom has much to do with it. What you will need to do is discreetly examine the producer's motives: find out where he's coming from and where he intends to go to. What are his reasons for the interview and what does he intend to ask?

Most interviews are to gather information or pull in a comment or reaction. Outside of politics, few set out to trap an interviewee or set them up for a fall. That said, on most occasions you will face the almost mandatory devil's advocate question to test your side of the argument. If you are prescribing a proposal or point of view, expect it to be contradicted. But come what may, you need to be prepared by finding out to the best of your ability what you're letting yourself in for.

If you haven't already got the facility to record your telephone conversations you should install one. That way you'll have a record of what was *actually* said, not just the impression you got from the conversation. Most dictation machines will take an induction mike. You simply stick it on the handset by its rubber sucker, plug it into your recorder and go. Induction mikes cost next to nothing and can save your face as well as your fortune.

Phone calls like these are seldom expected. They can catch you on the hop. When one comes, work your way through the following checklist until you are satisfied that you understand the motive and purpose of the interview:

- First get the name, title, company name, phone number and extension of your caller.
  Then you'll need answers to the following questions:

For all the media:

- What is the interview about?
- Why do you particularly want to talk to us/me?
- What angle do you intend to take?
  (This is to find out the *purpose* of the piece, whether the aim is for information or confrontation.)
- Who *exactly* would you like to speak to?
- Why that person in particular?
- Where did you get this story from?
  (If the source is a cutting you haven't read, ask them to fax it through or read it to you.)
- Who else are you planning to interview for the item?
  (Try to find out whether opponents of your case will be asked to give their views. If so:

  – will they have access to our comments before they are interviewed?
  – could we have access to theirs, so we can answer their case?)
- When do you want to do the interview?
- Where?
- How long will it take?
- When will it appear?

Then, if your caller is from TV or radio:

- Do you want to record the interview, or do it live?
- What programme will it go out on?
- Could you tell me the date and time of transmission?
- What form will the finished item take?
  – will it be a straight interview, one of several in a report; or part of a documentary?
- How long will the finished item run to?
  – how long is *our/my* contribution in it expected to run?
- Who will be conducting the interview?

If other interviewees are involved:

- In what order will the interviews be run?
- Will we all get equal airtime?

If it is in a studio:

- Where should we go?
- What time should we arrive?
- Who should we ask for?
- How long will you require us?

Finally for all the media:

- Could you just remind me again, of the areas you intend to cover in the interview?
  – and could you give me an idea of the first question, so I can prepare?

The checklist above is fairly comprehensive. Different questions will be appropriate under different circumstances. In any event, before you agree to the interview you should be certain that it's in your organisation's best interests, that it is within your policy and what you are likely to say follows your official line, and that it would reach a suitable target audience. You will need to consider whether to push to be interviewed live, of which more in a moment. Come what may, you should keep them talking until you're satisfied that giving the interview would be to your advantage.

You should also be aware of the consequences of *declining* to give the interview:

- Will your case be left unrepresented?
- Will criticisms go undefended?
- Will the company image suffer as a result?
- Will an opportunity be lost?
- Will a rival gain mileage instead?

I would never begin a conversation with a journalist without saying, 'What's the story you're writing, and who else are you talking to?' to get a feel of it.

Des Wilson, General Election Campaign Director, Liberal Democrats

Ask yourself: 'What is the interview all about? Why is *this* newspaper contacting *me*? Why are they asking about *this* story? What is it they want to *know*?'

John Bryant, *The European*

Motive

The first and last questions on that checklist should give you a good idea of what they're really after from the interview. Those questions don't simply accept the request at face value. 'What angle do you intend to take?' goes beyond the subject matter and politely questions motive, reason and approach.

Source

Where did you get this story from? will give you an even better idea of where they're coming from. TV and radio still take many of their leads from the newspapers and specialist magazines, who have more troops on the ground and more column inches to fill.

If they've taken their lead from a cutting, you should already be aware of it. If you missed the cutting, it is unlikely you will be able to get hold of a copy within the next twenty minutes, so ask them to fax it to you or, failing that, read it to you over the phone. Then you can see the angle of the original story, catch up on any new developments and get a clearer idea of where this interview would be coming from.

We have a précis of all the cuttings about the energy industry on our desk at eight o'clock in the morning. We get a feel of the style and persuasion of the different correspondents who write regularly about our business.

John Pike

Every company of any stature should subscribe to a press cuttings service which will keep you informed about what the media is saying about you and your competition. The same applies to pressure groups and their opposition. As we know, information is power.

News begets news. Despite the immediacy of broadcasting all news and current affairs programmes will study the newspapers and will often follow what is being said in their columns. Specialist programmes will subscribe to specialist magazines and look to them for leads about what they should be covering. So if you're keeping up with the press and current events you should have a shrewd idea of the sort of questions they are likely to be put to you.

Preview Material

The TV company may want to introduce some other footage into the interview – a video by way of illustration or a taped interview giving another person's point of view. Ask them if you can preview any other material which they intend to use in the report. They don't have to agree, but if they do, it's to your clear advantage.

If they won't show you the material, you need to discreetly find out why? Why do they want to keep it under wraps? Are they trying to catch you out or trap you? You can hardly ask them that, but it should be possible to work out their motive from their answers to the other questions.

The Line of Questions

Even while you're discussing the interview on the telephone, you should be quickly forming a clear idea of what it is that you want to get out of the interview and be reasonably confident that you'll succeed in that aim.

If the producer is vague about the actual questions he/she plans to ask, don't automatically smell a conspiracy; it might still be too early to have focused their thoughts beyond the actual news item to a specific line of questions. Yet he/she should, at this stage, have a general idea of the direction they want the interview to take, and it is more than reasonable that you are informed of that.

H they can't or won't be drawn, then say that obviously you need to know the kind of things they plan to ask so you can prepare for the interview, and say you'll call them back in twenty minutes when they can give you a clearer idea. Don't commit yourself until you're satisfied.

It is unrealistic to press for a list of the actual questions in advance.

> I *never* tell anyone what the specific questions are that I'm going to ask them. Apart from anything else, it's practically impossible to know how the interview is going to go. But I think they're entitled to know the subject areas and what the interview is about. They're *not* entitled to specific ammunition... and I think you're very ill-advised if you don't find that out first before you go into an interview.
> Jeremy Paxman, Presenter, *Newsnight*, BBC2

You don't give them the questions, because the questions depend on their answers.

Bud Evans

Even if someone were to present you with a list of questions – and no self-respecting producer would do such a thing – there's no guarantee they or their reporter will keep to them. Only a poor interviewer will stick slavishly to the brief. A good one will use it as a guide. He or she will argue correctly that the questions need to be fluid and unscripted so they can respond to what is said. And because you represent a vested interest, you can be sure that the reporter will always ask a devil's advocate question to test your case against the other side of the argument – and that is hardly going to be revealed to you before the game begins.

The *best* way to anticipate their line of questioning is to put yourself in their shoes. What would *you* ask if you were conducting the interview? The sort of things a reporter will want to find out are:

- What's happening *now*?
- What's new?
- How will it affect the audience?
- What's the scale of it?
- What are its advantages/disadvantages?
- And what happens next?

Those are basic questions to gauge the facts of a story and its impact and significance.

Reporters are always searching for the relevance of a news item to their audience. That audience will vary from programme to programme. If you're invited to give an interview about your new automated assembly line to *Union World*, the presenter would focus on the impact this would have on union members: the number of jobs lost, changes in working conditions and retraining programmes. The same subject covered by *Business Daily* might look at savings made; productivity increased; quality improved and other questions that businesspeople will want answered.

One consoling piece of advice is that usually the reporter is unlikely to be an expert on the story. Special correspondents are the exception rather than the rule. So you will usually know far more about the story than the reporter. You should also be well versed in what your critics are saying. But beware of complacency – the smiling piranha sizing you up could just surprise you by turning out to be a world authority.

So it's well worth finding out who will be doing the grilling. But if your inquisitor doesn't have the special correspondent tag, you can breathe more easily – perhaps.

Know Your Media

As was said earlier, it is important to be familiar with the specialist TV and radio programmes that cover your area of interest, so you'll understand their format and style and know what to expect. You can hardly keep the producer waiting a week while you watch the next edition before you make a decision. It is useful to hold a recent video or tape recording of each of them so you can quickly prepare yourself for their way of working.

Documentary programmes particularly can take some months to come to air. If you are in any doubt that the information you plan to give will still hold true by the time the programme is transmitted, you'll need to get an undertaking that if circumstances alter significantly, the TV company will let you record a fresh interview.

There are limits to how much you can demand. This is the BBC's advice to its own producers:

> The BBC does not surrender editorial control over its output...
> Programme makers are expected to deal firmly with
> contributors who misconstrue courtesy and cooperation as the
> concession of editorial control. It is up to editors to decide
> which conditions imposed by a contributor cannot be accepted
> because they would invalidate the contribution.
> *BBC Guidelines for Factual Programmes*[4]

And the Independent Television Commission also spells it out:

> Sometimes, interviewees – including spokesmen for the
> government – will seek to impose their own conditions on the
> conduct and use of their interview. Such requests are not
> improper in themselves, but care should be taken to ensure that

39

what is included ... is determined by criteria of journalistic impartiality and not as the result of pressure.

ITC Programme Code[5]

Be Available

Speed is essential. Where incorrect information or half-truths are circulating it is vital to put the record straight *quickly*.

David Morgan Rees[6]

Availability is crucial. The sell-by date of news is always *now*. The bane of every news producer is a contact who is not available, or is 'in a meeting'.

Sometimes you know you're being sidelined – they're in meetings, they don't bother to ring back, their secretaries don't pass on the messages. The longer they delay the less chance their account will get into the paper.

We would carry the story anyway, and just say they were unavailable. We'll rarely drop a story if it's good enough, simply because we can't get hold of somebody. We would just go to another source to stand it up.

Russell Hotten

If it's an important story and someone just doesn't want to do it then we'll do it with an analyst or even with our own experts.

Andrew Clayton

People who don't reply to calls are obviously not doing themselves any good in terms of public relations. Even if they prefer to say nothing, it is in their interest to return a call and let us know, because journalists are only human, and if you continually don't return your calls, it creates the possibility of some ill-will.

John Bryant

If you have a growing suspicion that an interview will work to your disadvantage, play for time and arrange to call them back within twenty minutes – and then keep to your word. Producers and reporters are impatient people. They *earn* their ulcers. They always have a deadline looming and a list of story angles to follow, and you represent just one of several possibilities. If you don't bite, they'll take their fishing elsewhere.

If you're given the chance to get your message across to an audience of perhaps millions, then drop what you're doing and take it. Your window of opportunity will not stay open indefinitely, so be flexible.

Return messages. If you're in a meeting, come out of it unless it's a matter of life and death, and even then keep your secretary posted as to when you'll be free. It means you might have to change your carefully timetabled routine to fit in with the media and turn what is always an untimely interruption into a welcome opportunity. It is curious how some people will pull out the stops to address an audience of a couple of hundred, yet baulk at the offer of a top-drawer audience of millions:

A former director of a national consumer watchdog was addressing a conference in Edinburgh and had some very bitter things to say about the way the banks were treating their customers. He was claiming they were using vulnerable technology and expected punters to shoulder the risk and that their interest rates were more usurous than anywhere else in the world. The *Today* programme called him at 11.30pm after he had finished speaking and invited him to give a live interview in the morning. Instead of jumping at the chance he gulped hard, and protested, 'But I haven't gone to bed yet!' The producer offered to send a car round to him at 6.30 am. And eventually he agreed. But he nearly blew it.

Bud Evans

Who Should Do It?

The value to the company is huge. If you have a director who can handle an interview, who is confident and has the skill to put across the company message, then when you see these things being said on a television programme, it has much,

much more impact than advertising. Many people switch off to advertising, but there is a much better chance their attention will be held by what is being said this way.

John Pike

The media's choice of spokesperson might not be the most suitable person for the job. The media will insist on interviewing the Chairman when the Section Head may know far more about the subject and be an altogether livelier proposition. Your own choice should be whoever is best equipped to do the interview. You want an expert on the subject who is competent to speak; a skilled communicator; wise in the ways of the media and is available. This is a pretty tall order. It means that he or she will need to be trained. And it's no use holding off that crisis phone call to do that.

Fielding your own expert gives you more credibility, and the depth of their knowledge means they're less likely to be boxed into a corner by a sharp interviewer determined to show off how much he or she has mugged up on the subject.

And there's another spinoff. An articulate expert who's media-literate and *available* is a rare and valued contact in any journalist's little black book and it is highly likely that they would be called upon on other occasions to give interviews. Each time that happens, your organisation's name goes up in lights before a major audience. It is worth a company's while to invest in and cultivate such people.

But for the interview in question you might think it necessary to put forward somebody more senior. Or it might be your company's policy to protect senior management by using an information officer to give the interview. If you're uncertain whom to suggest, or their availability, play for time, and arrange to call them back *quickly*. Again, make sure you do.

If you're a company executive and you've been approached directly by the media, it probably means they've found a way of circumventing the press office. Put them on hold, and go back to press office to take their advice before you risk your reputation.

We're keen that whoever speaks for the company is somebody who has some overall say.

Andrew Clayton

42

We want the most important person we can get. It's always better for a national paper – in this case international – to talk to somebody at the top.

John Bryant

It's no use sending the office boy along to do the job.

Philip Ditton

Conversely:

If a company has been taken over, we may well want to go to the ground floor workers to try to get a comment on what impact it's had on the shop floor. We find that managers will lay down the law and refuse to let their workforce talk – that's a shame.

Russell Hotton

Qualities

There could be millions of listeners or viewers out there. Whoever is speaking for the company must speak with authority and confidence and know his subject inside out, using all his skill to put it over succinctly.

Philip Ditton

Your paragon will also need to be an attractive personality; the sort of person you're happy to let loose on an unsuspecting public. Looks are not terribly important, unless they are so gruesome as to be distracting. If somebody is obviously unphotogenic, if you put them up in front of a TV camera, the audience will react to them rather than respond to their message. But the same person may perform very well on the radio.

For television interviews in particular, it pays to be certain that whomever you put up to speak is an effective television performer. However satisfied *you* may be with a person's cheekbones, credibility and affable nature, there is no guarantee they will come over as well as you imagine on screen.

The camera is a distorting mirror and surprisingly capricious in whom it favours. It sees things rather differently to us. The only way to tell if someone has camera appeal is to put them up in front of one, preferably in a well-lit studio, and record the results. You may be surprised how some quite attractive faces can become disappointingly bland, and how features that you might have thought ordinary can suddenly sparkle. You will also understand why the Chinese call Westerners big-noses.

Looks are one thing, presentation ability is another. Obviously you should avoid setting up as a spokesman anyone with a lisp or a stammer or who drones in a monotone. The style, as well as the appearance should be lively and attractive.

If you expect to appear on TV in the near future, the best advice is to book up a practice session with your company's information office or with a media consultant and view the results yourself. Your advisors may be critical, but you are likely to be the harsher judge. Don't be hypercritical, though. For every professional TV presenter whose looks can turn heads there are several more who have found their way onto the screen because their hard-earned skills outweigh any natural assets.

Live or Recorded?

There's much debate over whether you should agree to give a recorded interview or, given the option, press for a live appearance:

> Any sensible person on a sensitive matter would insist on it being live. Now that's very inconvenient, you may have to go to a studio when you might not want to. But if you really want to do it, and they really want to have you, 'live' gives *you* control of the interview; whereas when you are edited, *they* have control. I have known occasions when I've done a half an hour interview and the trick question was at the end; it wasn't what you thought it was about, and that was the only thing that was used.
>
> Tony Benn, MP

Almost all pre-recorded interviews *are* edited in one form or another. But most people don't have malice aforethought, so I don't think that's anything to worry about. You can always get round that by agreeing to do a live interview.

Jeremy Paxman

A self-confident minister prefers, if possible, to be interviewed on television because, although the questions may be tough, he can fight back and the viewer sees it all, especially if the broadcast is live. There is no room for selection, condensation, tendentious editing, or running commentary; what is said is what the viewer gets, neither more nor less, and if the questioning is clearly unfair or aggressive, the minister will get the sympathy of the audience. With press interviews the risks are much greater.

Paul Johnson, *The Spectator*[7]

Recorded interviews can be boiled down to nothing, but live interviews can sometimes be dropped under the pressure of time or competition from a bigger breaking news story or one with better pictures. Frustrating for the professional who plans his diary months in advance and has to clear it at a moment's notice to make way for a TV appearance that fails to materialise:

The managing director of an engineering firm accepted an invitation to appear in a TV discussion programme going out live the following day. Arriving at the TV studio at 11 am after clearing his business diary and motoring a considerable distance, he was kept waiting for half and hour. Half an hour later, after the so-called 'preliminary' discussion, he was suddenly told the item in which he hoped to appear was cancelled.

The headline business, CBI/Abbey Life

Time, we know, is money. Put it that way, you have risked £500 worth of your time for £25,000 worth of promotion. Just write it off as the deal that got away.

If in Doubt...

If you finally decide to turn down a request for an interview, do it in such a way that you won't get struck off their contacts book. Apologise. Be honest about your reasons, without giving away any secrets. Be as helpful as you can in every other way, Offer to give them an interview at a later date, if you can. Do your darnedest to avoid them coming out with the line: 'we asked the company to comment, but they declined.' Let them know that there's an open door if they want to call you again some other time.

Masterclass

Tony Benn, MP for Chesterfield

The purpose of doing these things is to get a case across, [so] first find out what areas they want to cover, because they might want to interview you about something you didn't want to be interviewed about. You might feel you didn't have anything useful to say, that it might be open to misunderstanding, that it might open up things you weren't keen to open up,

The second thing is to enquire about the *purpose* of the programme. That's a little bit different, because the *areas* might relate only to your own interview, whereas the purpose of the programme might be quite separate from your own interests, and you could be fitted into a programme in a way which showed you up at a disadvantage.

Next ask, 'Who else are you going to interview?' so that you've got a feel for that and it will give you an indication,

Think about the likely objectives of the interviewer, so you are able to anticipate. I know for example, if there is a row in the Labour Party I will get nine telephone calls asking me would I be interviewed, and I will say 'No!' because I don't want to be in their little black book: 'if there's a row in the Labour party ring Mr Benn.'

I find if I refuse, which I do quite regularly to do a particular programme, they can't understand it. They think you would die rather than miss a chance to be on the air, but I say I'm awfully sorry, but it wouldn't be appropriate; it's not a subject I particularly want to deal with. But media people assume that you would go a hundred miles just to do half a minute.

John Pike, Manager Media Affairs, Shell UK

There are some [television and radio] programmes that you probably wouldn't touch at all, because you know they are there totally for entertainment value and not really for the business of informing people. And there are some programmes that you don't appear on anyway, because there is a very high chance you would be on a beating to nothing.

If you look at the track record of the programme and find that they do not really give the interviewee an opportunity to put his case; if you feel they are in the business of heavy editing; if you'd had bad experiences before with certain programmes, as I have, where they have used a pair of scissors to put my man's answers to different questions, then you give it a wide berth.

You don't have to be too worried about saying, I'm sorry we can't come along and appear on your show. It is better to see an empty seat and hear 'Shell was not prepared to come along here today,' than see somebody sitting in it for twenty minutes being screwed up.

Andrew Clayton, Editor, Business Daily, *Channel 4*

There are two sorts of item that we do: either a straight interview which lasts about two minutes, or an interview which is going to be put in a package. In other words, the reporter will lead the subject on from the various bits of the interview that we use.

For the first sort we'll use three or four answers; for the second we're looking for thoughts which are 20 to 25 seconds long.

WOULD YOU TELL AN INTERVIEWEE THE LENGTH OF MATERIAL YOU WOULD BE EXPECTING?

Yes, we would. We'd tell him what was being done with it because then he knows how to do it. There's no point conducting an interview with someone who's expecting to be able to talk on for ten minutes and finds it only lasts for two, because you won't cover the ground you're hoping to cover.

Des Wilson, General Election Campaign Director, Liberal Democrats

You can normally guess what they're *really* after. I had a phone call from The 'X' Diary, purporting to be interested in how advanced our General Election plans were. But the questions he kept asking were about what personalities I was planning to field during the election.

It quickly became clear that what he was looking for was a bit of gossip about who's in and who's out. So I challenged him directly and said, 'Well, you've rang about *this*, but are you in fact interested in *this*? Yes or No?' This embarrassed him and he more or less had to concede the point. I said, 'I don't mind discussing that, but I want to know what the story is you're writing.' Normally a journalist will tell you, and normally they'll be honest.

There have been occasions when I've been telephoned under the guise of one story and it's turned out to be another. But increasingly, in politics anyway, you deal with the same people repeatedly, and there's a more honest and direct relationship because they know they have to establish relationships that work.

HOW DO YOU GET INTO THE MIND OF A JOURNALIST TO ANTICIPATE THEIR AGENDA?

You need to know what the story is and what the context is in which you're being interviewed. Is this something in which I'm going to be the only one quoted, or am I going to be one paragraph amongst many. It's important, because if you've only got one paragraph, you've got to ask yourself, 'What's the most important thing I want to say here?'

HOW EFFECTIVE CAN AN INTERVIEW BE IN AFFECTING EVENTS? CAN YOU SELECT ONE WHICH HAS BEEN SIGNIFICANT TO YOU IN TERMS OF PUBLIC REACTION?

Back in the late 1960s Simon Dee had an hour-long live chat show on Sunday nights. It was the peak hour programme of the week, with one of the biggest audiences.

Normally they had on showbusiness people, but I went on when I was director of Shelter [the charity for the homeless]. For someone to come on and talk about a serious problem – the homeless – for 12 minutes at peak time, out of the context of the programme itself made a huge impact, in terms of money, support and publicity generated.

I learned from that how invaluable it can be to discuss serious topics on programmes that are not normally serious. It explains, incidentally, why politicians are often keen to go on chat show programmes like Wogan or Jimmy Young.

3

PREPARING THE INTERVIEW

The whole business with a programme is the struggle for the agenda. *They* want to get something out of you. *You* want to use the opportunity.

Work out what you want to say *before* the interview. I work it out quite simply. If I do *Question Time* and I have access to six million people for one fifth of an hour I will work out with *enormous* care what I want to get across.

Tony Benn

Prepare. You wouldn't want to embarrass yourself before a handful of friends, so why risk it with a million viewers? Never stroll into a studio with only the smug conviction that you can hack it. There are few media manipulators more accomplished than Tony Benn, and he admits to working hard to keep it that way. If Mr Benn has to prepare, then so must you. However great your expertise and understanding of your subject, you will still need to distil it into a message that will suit the media.

The biggest mistake company spokesmen tend to make is that they haven't really thought out what they are going to say – the opportunity that the interview gives them. You must know absolutely what it is that *you* want to get out of the interview.

Bud Evans

Identify the two or three key points you want to get across and I don't mean 20 or 30. If it's a rapidly changing situation, make sure you know the up-to-date position. If it is a matter of facts, make sure you know the facts. If it is a matter of opinion, make sure you *have* one. It's amazing the number of people you would expect to have opinions who don't!

Alison Sergeant

The advice that follows is geared towards the broadcast medium but is eminently adaptable to print.

The Message

The most important thing – and this goes for *all* interviews, of any kind, anywhere – is to ask yourself, 'Why am I doing this; what is the purpose of it; what am I trying to achieve here?' And be clear what it is and what you need to say to do that.

Des Wilson

This interview is taking place because either you've gone looking for publicity, or the media has come looking for you. Let's clear up one misconception right from the start. Assuming it was your handout that started things rolling, and a reporter is bending your ear for an interview, the interview will be about the news release – right? Wrong! The news release is simply the starting point _. the pump primer. Journalism targets moving stories. One of its basic demands is to take a news story further. Your carefully worded news release has given them the *facts* but now they want to know what all journalists always want to know: Who; What; When; Where; Why and How?

To help yourself prepare your message put yourself in *their* shoes and anticipate their questions. That way, what you say will be what they want to hear, and you'll be able to get your message across without having to appear on camera wearing a sandwich board.

The art of media communication is to marry your message with their needs. And remember, it's not the producer or reporter whose needs you are addressing, but the audience or readership they are working for. Two words of caution. Before you do anything, first check the company line. What use is a brilliant performance if you cut across company policy and it costs you your career? Next, don't be over-ambitious. Broadcasting is a medium of impressions.

Someone once said, 'half of what you say gets twisted, the rest gets forgotten – so keep it simple.'

The spoken word is fleeting. The best you can hope for is to leave your audience with one clear impression, and to do that whether you are a businessman, a politician or a pressure group, as we said earlier, your message has to have impact:

15,000 people in New York City alone have died of Aids today. This is appalling. These figures are appalling. These facts are appalling. And they are easily understood by anyone sitting at home watching the television news. Anyone who picks up a newspaper, anyone who listens to the radio. Those facts have to be presented to those people.

Chip Ducket, ACT-UP[1]

Regardless of the media agenda, you have to be certain of what you want to achieve. Like Chip Ducket of ACT-UP, you need a well-defined objective – one clear idea that, come what may, you are going to leave in the minds of your audience. And if it's going to lodge, it will need a hook.

To find the right hook for your message, US communications specialist Milo O. Frank suggests asking yourself the following questions:

- What's the most unusual part of your subject?
- What's the most interesting; exciting; dramatic and humorous part?
- Identify each part clearly and work on expressing it until you can boil each part down to a single sentence.[2]

That sentence should combine simplicity, clarity and impact – and be of particular interest to your audience:

Lockerlie Lighting *must* be allowed to build a new factory – 300 jobs depend on it.

Start with your conclusion and then introduce evidence that will prove your point. It may not be the way most company reports are written, but it is the most basic rule of newswriting.

Shades of light and dark and subtlety of argument will be lost on the audience. That's not to insult their intelligence – it's just to recognise the limitations of a medium that's so fleeting it can't even be used to wrap tomorrow's fish and chips. Whether the item is a 20 second comment for a news bulletin, or a 30 minute documentary, the aim is the same – to leave the audience with one clear impression – your message.

So make your message short, relevant and crystal clear.

If you want to make it memorable, then consider building in one (or, two) snappy one-liners:

'...like being savaged by a dead sheep.'
Chancellor Denis Healey of Sir Geoffrey Howe, 1978

'...short, sharp, shock.'
Home Secretary William Whitelaw, 1979 after W. S. Gilbert, 1885

'On your bike.'
Adapted from a remark by Employment Secretary Norman Tebbit, 1981

Colourful, pointed and imaginative phrases are an odds-on bet to be used as sound bites. But make sure they're *relevant...*

Everything you say, one-liners included, will have to support your message. Nothing must distract from it. Unless you get that message across, you'll have failed and your opportunity will be lost. But when you realise how little you need to say, it all becomes that much simpler.

Key Points and Pointers

You're the expert. Given time and the inclination, you could probably write a book on your subject. But whatever your inclination, they won't give you the time. To get your message up in lights where the world will be able to see it clearly you will have to reduce your argument ruthlessly down to two or three key points. *No more.* And that holds true no matter how complex or convoluted the issue in question.

Whatever the subject, you will need to prepare a good, strong case that can be presented comfortably in just two minutes – less if that's all they're offering. Your key points should be strong and simple arguments that have something positive to declare. For each key point you will need two or three pointers – simple facts that back up your case and drive your message home. You should be able to state each key point and each pointer in a *single* sentence. See how the key points and pointers build up the message below:

Message

Lockerlie Lighting *must* be allowed to build a new factory.

Key points

1. Lockerlie Lighting is making record profits.

Pointers

- Profits are up by 50 per cent.
- Export orders are the highest ever.
- Profit sharing means all the staff are better off.

2. The business needs to expand.

- We need to build a new factory to cope with demand.
- This will create 300 new jobs for local people.
- More jobs will follow if trade continues to grow.

3. We must succeed in getting planning permission.

- Business can't stand still, we have to expand to survive.
- Competitors are snapping at our heels.
- Townspeople have made Lockerlie a success, we're grateful, and with the new factory we can go from strength to strength.

In a two minute interview, these are the points you will need to get across. But if you know only a single comment will be chosen, or you are appearing as one of many voices in a discussion programme, get your priority point across immediately, don't lead into it – you might never get there.

TV interviews are the opposite of court cases where you hear all the evidence before coming to a verdict. You may not get time to conclude your evidence, so you have to put your message across with alacrity.

If a short comment is all that's required, then you'll have to get your message over in a single statement lasting about 20 seconds:

> We're making record profits and export orders are their highest ever, so we *need* this new factory. It'll mean 300 new jobs to start with and more later. All we need now is planning permission. Lockerlie Lighting is a profit sharing company and our workforce is local, so the new factory can only be good news for the town.

This gets the message across by condensing the three main points. It also spells out clearly the all important 'What's in it for the audience' angle, of which more in a moment. When comments come in short chunks like this they're known as *sound bites*.

A word of warning: never qualify your arguments – develop them instead. The process of editing usually removes qualifying phrases and other awkward clauses. Arguments become streamlined for simplicity and to save time. This means shades of grey can become black and white and the elaborate picture you are painting can be reduced to a cartoon with a few bold outlines. Don't fight it. Prepare a simple message that needs no qualification.

As far as Lockerlie Lighting is concerned, your objective is clear – to press the case for planning permission. You intend to do so by winning the hearts and minds of your audience by showing them that what's good for Lockerlie Lighting is good for them.

Some psychology has been employed here in not beginning with what for your company is the main issue – the need to win planning permission. Instead, you begin with a positive news angle that is good news for your employees. But again, you can only do that if you know you will be given time to get all your points home. If there is *any* doubt, go straight in with it.

What's in it for me?

Notice how each point dangles a golden thread before the audience. This is the 'what's in it for me' angle, where the 'me' is not you but your audience. This golden thread should run throughout your message, picking out the positive benefits of what you have to say to those who will hear it.

Every interview must have a 'what's in it for me' angle. Without it the issue becomes irrelevant and therefore not newsworthy. It's back to the market again, to matching your wants with their needs – what *you* want to say with what they want to hear. And the middleman in this market is the producer.

Let's return to those key points above. If you read between the lines, each has its golden thread:

1. Lockerlie Lighting is making record profits.

- Profits are up by 50 per cent.
- Export orders are the highest ever.
- Profit sharing means *all* the staff are better off.

The golden thread in the first is: What's good for Lockerlie Lighting is good for you.

2. The business needs to expand.

- We need to build a new factory to cope with demand.
- This will create 300 new jobs for local people.
- More jobs will follow if trade continues to grow.

The golden thread in the second is: A new factory for *us* means more jobs for *you*.

3. We must succeed in getting planning permission.

- Business can't stand still, we must expand to survive.
- Competitors are snapping at our heels.
- Townspeople have made Lockerlie a success, we're grateful, and with the new factory we can go on from strength to strength.

Here, the golden thread for your audience is: You have everything to gain from granting planning permission, and everything to lose by refusing.

These implicit threads interweave and combine to make a message that is explicit – the opinion you want to pass on to everyone in your audience: Lockerlie Lighting must be allowed to build a new factory.

You and the journalist want the same thing from the interview. Both of you want to leave the audience with a clear impression of what the story is about. Where you may differ is in your perception of the substance of the story itself. That is why running through the pre-interview checklist is so important. You have to get into the mind of the journalist.

You may be able to influence that perception, even alter it, but you are unlikely to be able to overturn it. And in the end, it is the journalist's perception that will prevail and determine how the story is to be presented.

Having influenced your utmost, you will need to respond with material that will fit the interviewer's perception, if you are to respond at all. Unless there is that match, what you say will be edited to fit, or discarded.

The ideal story is one which will have them leaning on the bar in the evening saying to their mates: 'Did you see that story about Lockerlie Lighting on the box – there's going to be a new factory and more jobs – if the council doesn't stick its ruddy oar in.' Few in the audience will remember all of the story or even most of it, but the majority of the audience should be able to sum up the point of the story in a single sentence. You want the one impression they're left with to be the single impression you set out to give them – your message.

Your message, each key point and each pointer, must be capable of being understood perfectly and instantly by someone who has absolutely no knowledge of your subject. Time flies. Most inexperienced interviewees prepare far too much material. Remember, you may be given as little as 15 seconds to get your message across. Whether you've 15 seconds or 15 minutes, you *have* to get your message over in that time.

Making Notes

> Notes are fine as long as they're not too obvious. If they are, the audience notices it straightaway – absolutely straightaway. They see the man doing it and their reaction is, 'Oh gosh, he clearly hasn't got the information at his fingertips.'
>
> Andrew Clayton

If you have to take notes into the interview keep them down to a summary of the key points and their pointers. You should be able to get your notes onto a filecard. This must be kept out of sight of any camera, so produce headings that are large enough and clear enough to be able to take in at a glance without holding up the page.

Notes are a safety net only – an *aide memoire* – under no circumstances should you read from a prepared statement during the interview. If you must use notes, make sure you glance down only when you are being asked a question as this is when the camera is more likely to be off you. If the camera catches you you'll look ill-prepared and shifty, as though you can't bear to meet the interviewer's eye.

You may be given time to develop on your theme, but you should use that to focus on the points before you rather than to introduce new information. Your audience is unlikely to remember anything more. Don't be fooled into thinking you need lots of material in case you run out of things to say. You're the expert, you know your subject inside out and from your list of three key points it should be easy for you to talk for up to 20 minutes about the issue you know so well and have rehearsed so thoroughly.

Instead of adding to the information, reinforce it. Find different ways of reiterating it to drive the point home with examples and anecdotes.

Anticipate Difficult Questions

> For *Any Questions*, I read all the newspapers for the week and almost always I get every question in advance out of a list of about 60.
>
> Tony Benn

3. Preparing the Interview

There it is again: preparation. It's vital that you go into an interview well-briefed and confident that if the worst comes you can turn it to good. There are two sides to every issue. Your task is to promote a point of view. The journalist's task is to test your argument the same way steel is tempered: by banging it hard with a blunt instrument – in this case with contradictory facts or opinions.

News is often about controversy. So if you're invited to appear on a news programme, the chances are that you have something controversial to say. If so, expect the point of contention to be the focus of the interview and brace yourself for it. As political journalist Paul Foot puts it: 'news and political broadcasting bores its audience off the air as soon as it slides from controversy into public relations.'

Where you anticipate dealing with difficult questions, your aim is to prepare answers that will effectively:

- counter the argument;
- reassure the audience; and
- promote your company.

So be certain that:

- you've recognised all the points that might be contentions, and
- you've rehearsed how to deal with them.

Don't skimp on rehearsal or skip over it because it might be embarrassing. It would be far more embarrassing to find yourself mouthing like a goldfish during a live TV interview.

Rehearsal

Quite a large percentage of the time they launch into you and come up with the unexpected. You have to make sure that the person who is going to be interviewed is competent to handle himself.

Before you give the interview sit the prospective interviewee down and go through the list covering possible angles. Test him out in a question and answer session.

Sometimes you will need to put him on the ropes a bit, giving him probably as bad as he could expect in the studio.

John Pike

Having drawn up your key points, the aim of your rehearsal is to find the most effective way of putting them across in the time available. And that means practice. And not just on paper. Rehearse it in a mirror. Tell it to a tape recorder. Get a colleague who's good at playing devil's advocate to put you through your paces, or sign up for a training session.

Get your sparring partner to test every weakness in the argument by putting over strongly the opposing point of view and contradictory evidence. If you expect a tough time have a second colleague sit in on the rehearsal to offer suggestions, and keep practising until you can fend off every argument coolly and succinctly.

You can't afford to face the cameras with an idea that has got no further than your imagination. Get it out in the open where you can *hear* it. But be careful: while you must be certain of the facts there's no merit in learning lines. You'll find that you won't be able to deliver them as planned, and you'll be so fixed on trying to remember them as you've rehearsed them that your delivery will probably be stilted and hesitant. A good interview has an air of spontaneity about it so avoid rehearsing it to death. You'll need some adrenalin to make your interview sparkle.

Presentation

A survey carried out by American psychologists has found that a quarter to one third of what appears on television is misunderstood by viewers.

The headline business, CBI/Abbey Life[3]

As you consider how to present your case, remember to be mindful of your audience. You're not addressing a boardroom, or discussing technicalities with like-minded colleagues. When you appear on TV or radio you are BROADcasting. You are the specialist – they are the laymen. The journalist's role is to act as mediator between the two of

60

you. If you can appreciate that task you'll be able to present your case more effectively with less need for intervention by the reporter.

Below are the key points to watch out for:

Assume No Prior Knowledge from the Audience

Even though you're immersed in your business and your product, your audience may have no concept of it at all- unless, of course, you're appearing on a specialist programme with a dearly defined target audience. Tabloid newspapers are written with the vocabulary of the average 12 year old. And they're the most widely read press in Britain. Assume your audience doesn't understand your subject, but is willing to learn, and set out to explain it to them but without being patronising. The moment an audience suspects you of talking to the tops of their heads, you'll find yourself addressing their backs.

Likewise, the insecure can sometimes attempt to hide behind the barricades of their own expertise. Never be tempted to blind people with science to show them how smart you are. They will simply sneer at you for having your head in the clouds.

Avoid Jargon

The best that can be said of jargon is that it is a specialist language. As such it is manifestly inappropriate to the *broad*caster. At worst, jargon is the language of the initiated. It is to show you are in and they are out. If you hide yourself behind it you will also conceal your message. Your audience will probably be neither specialists nor initiates, so avoid acronyms or abbreviations or any technical language. In fact, don't use any long words where short and simple ones will do. What may be everyday English in your workplace could be 'gobbledygook' to outsiders.

The acid test is this: would your mother understand you? Not many mothers (or anyone else, for that matter) would claim to make sense of the following, adapted by the CBI from an actual news release and waved as a warning for PR people:

> Intrinsic safety certification, according to CENELEC standards has been granted to the Wonderbar Xynophone 56 range of gearless pressure transmitters, giving them a clearance for erection throughout the EEC in situations where protection levels appropriate to AAy-ia-twc-p3 are specified.[4]

Even the trade press might have trouble with that one. However, that example was sent to a mass-circulation newspaper. Fortunately, nobody would speak like that during an interview, would they...?

Take time to consider what you're going to say and take the trouble to translate everything into plain English, but be mindful of the following:

> Whilst translating polysyllabic and turbid locution into an idiom affording enhanced perspicacity, the perceptible augmentation of pellucidity may occasionally begat equivocalness, forfeiting as a consequence the narrative's verisimilitude; however any resultant decrementation of veracity must on no occasion be permitted to assume an amplitude whereby the communiqué is rendered fallacious.

Or to put it another way:

> Keep it simple, but avoid oversimplifying it to the point where it becomes misleading.

Simplify Figures

A similar word of warning about the use of figures. It's impossible for an audience to hear and take in any but the simplest of numbers. Figures are much easier to understand when read than when heard. Round them up or round them down, but keep them *simple*. Better to be vague and say, 'Almost a million pounds' than be precise and floor everyone with '£966,397'. Try not to use more than one figure in an interview, and if you simply must use fractions, keep them at kindergarten level. *Never* speak in decimals.

Explain Abstract Ideas

What you're saying has to make clear sense to your audience at first hearing. With a newspaper or magazine article, they can re-read it until they can get your drift, but in broadcasting there's no second chance. While they're puzzling over what you've just said, they're not listening to what you're saying now.

Hardest of all to communicate verbally are concepts, ideas and relationships. Broadcasting communicates by painting a picture in the minds of its audience. And the picture has to be something you can see – a solid, everyday object. Be descriptive. Engage the imagination. Always go for simplicity and clarity. Keep it human, keep it personal, keep it real.

An abstract idea is like the invisible man – you have to throw paint over him or dress him up before you can see him. S.I. Hayakawa explains this with his ladder of abstraction idea, which uses Bessie the cow as an example:

> To the cowhand, Bessie is a loveable old friend who gazes at him with her big brown eyes while she chews the cud. To a visitor, she is merely an old brown cow. To the farm manager, every cow on the farm is an item of livestock. To the bookkeeper, livestock comes under the heading of farm assets. To the accountant, assets are synonymous with wealth. Each step up the abstraction ladder take us one step further from faithful old Bessie.
>
> Ask someone to imagine a cow and they might picture a beast very different from Bessie; tell them 'livestock' and they could imagine a pig or a sheep; 'farm assets' could be tractors or ploughs; 'assets' could be anything saleable, and 'wealth' may simply conjure up a wad of notes. Poor old Bessie![5]

So when you're explaining your business, describe it in terms your audience will be able to picture immediately. If they can see it, they'll understand it.

Use Analogies

Everything you say needs to be brought down to a *human* scale to help your audience grasp it in the limited time available. Which gives you a clearer picture?

> The Stits Skybaby is 9 foot 10 inches in length and has a wingspan of 7 foot 2.

or:

> The Stits Skybaby really is a tiny aeroplane. To give you an idea of just how small: if you put 23 of them nose to tail, they still wouldn't measure up to a Jumbo Jet. And the wingspan is so tiny that an entire Stits could fit easily into the air intake of a single Jumbo Jet engine.

With something less visual than an aeroplane, analogy could be the only way to make sense of it:

> The world's most powerful volcanic eruption was at Tambora in Indonesia in 1815. The energy released was equivalent to 8 times 10 to the power of 19 joules.

Was it now? Unless you're a geologist you're unlikely to be any the wiser. How about this:

> The world's most powerful volcanic eruption was at Tambora in Indonesia in 1815. The energy released was 100 times greater than the most powerful nuclear test explosion the world has ever seen – or to put it another way, this one volcano was as potent as 300,000 Hiroshima atom bombs.

Journalists use analogies all the time to bring ideas down to a level to which people can relate. It doesn't take much homework to be able to play them at their own game.

Use Anecdotes

Good journalism has a lot in common with storytelling. To hold and keep an audience you have to speak their language and win their interest. As anyone who's had to endure after dinner speeches will know, a well-chosen anecdote, especially if it's amusing, can be the spoonful of sugar that helps the medicine go down. More than that, it can lower an audience's defences, win them over and help them to recall what you've said.

Anecdotes are stories about people. That means your audience will be able to relate to the message. Let's go back to Lockerlie Lighting:

> **Interviewer:** So presumably you took on more staff to cope with the demand?
> **Interviewee:** Yes, in fact we've doubled the workforce in just four years.

Alright as far as it goes, but it could be brought to life with a relevant anecdote:

> Yes, in fact we've doubled the workforce in just four years. Doris Melchett, for example, joined us when we first started as an assembly worker. Today she's a Deputy Manager and the entire Melchett family is on our payroll. Husband Robby runs the paint shop and daughters Doreen and Katy are doing what their mum did when she started work at Lockerlie Lighting. And there'll be more job opportunities when the council approves our expansion plans.

But remember, the media interview is not an after dinner speech. Use anecdotes sparingly, and only as supporting material; keep them short and keep them crisp.

Supplying Graphics

During a two minute television interview you'll be lucky to utter more than 300 words. A single graphic could save you a thousand words. Why waste your breath – and your airtime – when you could offer to provide a suitable illustration? And what more suitable for Lockerlie Lighting than an artist's impression of the proposed new extension?

If you think you have a suitable graphic, the media might want to adapt it to their style – especially if it has the company logo splashed rather too prominently all over it. A photograph will need to be roughly the proportion of the television screen, that is 4" wide by 3" high. Studio picture stands will take enlargements of up to 30 by 23 cm. If your shot is the size of a family snapshot, it'll probably be too small.

The TV station should be able to handle transparencies, and again, the larger the better. Footage from the corporate video could also be useful, to be run as it is or frozen as a still. Sound, basic shots of the premises and the process that are not so tightly edited that they can't be edited again are preferred. Clear it with the producer well beforehand and let him or her know exactly what's on offer and what video format you've used. Quality is paramount.

> We won't take graphics, because they won't be within our style. If a video is up to the required technical standard that's Betacam SP – then we can use it. But what we don't want is something which is cut around and has loads of commentary. We won't ever use that sort of thing.
>
> Andrew Clayton

Promote the Company Name – Carefully

Your TV or radio appearance may centre around some issue in the news, but it can be used as an opportunity to promote the company name. If you look at the examples above you'll find many make a point of pressing home the name. But beware of overdoing it. Radio and TV stations usually have strict rules about plugs.

> Don't emphasise the name of a firm or product visually or verbally beyond the editorial demands of a story.
>
> BBC Guidelines

We would not want them to plug themselves. We wouldn't want them to mention their product or their company name in the interview. We would agree that there should be a mention somewhere, in fairness to them, and that would probably be in the cue.

Bud Evans

If the company name is mentioned in the introduction to the interview then you ought to be satisfied. If it doesn't then one mention is often permissible. Two might be stretching goodwill. Three times and that could be your last appearance on air. Besides, the audience will cotton on that you're using the opportunity to gain cheap publicity.

Television reports may use a caption superimposed over the foot of your picture, naming both you and your organisation. This will stay on screen for about four seconds and is a stronger plug than any verbal namecheck. If you're in any doubt about where you stand, ask the producer to fill you in on the groundrules for namechecks. After all, what's in it for him is that you are there – what's in it for you is self-promotion.

On a *Woman's Hour* programme I compiled about the state of the British shoe industry, I was forbidden by my producer, on pain of death, to introduce one of my interviewees as a buyer from Marks and Spencer. She was introduced as a buyer 'from one of Britain's major high-street chains'. Not to be foxed, the buyer neatly sidestepped the problem by stating that 'thousands of pairs of shoes, *wrapped in our distinctive bright green shopping bags*, are sold in our stores every day.' That's ingenuity.

Dina Ross[6]

Foreign Language Interviews

Take Belgium – you've got the three key regions and they all hate each other. All the media are divided and you can get a totally different response from one paper to the next, depending on what language you speak. You need to use nationals who know the local media intimately.

Steve Ellis, Media Counsellor, Burson-Marsteller (PR Consultancy)

The more widespread your interest and the higher your profile, the more likely you are to be called upon to give an interview by the international media. Unless your knowledge of that language is very, very good – in other words a considerable advance upon schoolboy French – you would be well advised to ask them to interview you in English. Failing that, delegate the task or use an interpreter.

To the eternal shame of the English and eternal benefit of English speakers everywhere, many foreign viewers will understand them perfectly well without the need for subtitles. As Philip Ditton of the CBI puts it, 'Just think of all those people we've seen on our TV screens from Lithuania and all points east who suddenly come to life speaking perfect English.' Avoid finding yourself caught in the embarrassing and potentially damaging position of trying to answer questions whose subtlety escapes you because your knowledge of their language isn't good enough. Fortunately professional media organisations which frequently need to interview people from different countries will usually reflect a language mix among their staffs.

I think we could interview anybody in any language, but as English is now the *lingua franca* for much of the world I would say that businessmen who conduct their interviews in English generally have an advantage. We are interviewing all over the world and most of them are happy to be interviewed in English and do so very well.

But any businessman who feels that he is out of his depth being interviewed in any other language is foolish to try.

John Bryant

Foreign Perspectives

When an Englishman touches his thumb with his forefinger in the shape of a '0' he means 'OK'. If he makes the same gesture to a man in Japan it means 'money'. A Frenchman would interpret it as 'it's free', and the message he will convey to a Tunisian is 'I want to kill you'. Local knowledge is the key.

CBI

When it comes to giving an interview for the foreign media you'll need a clear understanding of *their* perspective on the news. The 'what's in it for me' angle holds as true as ever; it's just that the 'me' in question happens to be living in a different country.

If you're likely to find yourself in this position, then you'll need to keep abreast of what the foreign media is saying about you and your line of business. A cuttings service would help. Obviously it's not possible to be familiar with the style of every foreign news, current affairs and specialist programme, so what you may need is a media consultant from that country who can advise at short notice about whether or not to give that interview.

Approaches to interviewing can vary, too:

Compared to the French, the British [media] can be brutally direct. You are likely to be given a much more gentle time in France or Germany than you would in Britain, because of the harsher convention of tough interviewing in Britain.

Andrew Clayton

But with the rise of pan-European television and developing media connections, those differences are likely to diminish.

Masterclass

Bud Evans, an Editor of the Today programme, Radio 4

DO YOU FIND THAT CORPORATE SPOKESMEN UNDERSTAND HOW TO PREPARE THEIR MESSAGE TO ADDRESS THE NEWS AGENDA, OR ARE THEY OBLIVIOUS TO IT?

They tend not to see it clearly from any angle but their own. It's the old thing about politicians and spokesmen berating the press for covering what is to them an important story in a peculiar way, without appreciating the hours they've spent on it. Some of them don't want to see it from any other point of view. They want to think that their statement is the news because it is *their* statement.'

Russell Hotten, Business Editor, The Birmingham Post

One of the hassles of being a financial or business reporter is dealing with powerful people who don't take no for an answer and who are used to giving orders.

All of a sudden there's some journalist hungry for a good story who is asking *them* questions, advising them and directing them. It can come as a bit of a shock.

Occasionally, if a press release comes through from a company or directly from a chief executive, it might be awful and we won't use it. A couple of days later they'll ring and *demand* that we use it. And it's usually prefaced with, 'Do you know who I am? I'm the chief executive of X company...' Well, it just gets everybody's back up.

DO INTERVIEWEES SOMETIMES APPEAR UNPREPARED FOR YOUR QUESTIONS – DO YOU EVER CATCH THEM ON THE HOP?

Oh, all the time – although it's not done deliberately. Sometimes they don't expect the questions to be so frank and direct.

Tony Benn, MP

Take parliamentary questions. There you are facing a battery of different questioners, some hostile and some friendly. The same applies if you are doing an interview at a difficult moment. I would sit and say, 'Now what do you think they are going to ask?' Occasionally I have done television press conferences, and you know it will be Peter Jenkins and Anthony Howard, and you sit and think very, very, hard and usually you can anticipate questions.

But you shouldn't prepare detailed answers. It can be very stale if you have prepared long answers to questions, because an interview should have a vital spontaneous character which has to be preserved if it is going to be influential.

Philip Ditton, Chief Information Officer and Deputy Director of Public Relations, CBI

The Single European Market presents British industry with its biggest challenge and its biggest opportunity. I think companies are increasingly responding to this and are addressing themselves to the wider audience in Europe.

It is no use thinking you can get away with fractured French, because you can't. The best thing to do in those circumstances is to offer to give an interview in English, and leave the interviewer to do a voiceover and hope that will be acceptable. It *might* be. But he might go to another company down the road who've got a fluent French speaker.

John Bryant, Editor, The European

The onus should be on the media to sort it out. If we were interviewing a German businessman in English, I would still prefer to send a German-speaking English journalist, or an English-speaking German journalist, so they can lapse in and out of German should they wish.

It's always very impressive if the company can trot out someone who can put their case fluently in the language of the media concerned, but be *straightforward*: if you're phoned up by a foreign newspaper say, 'Look, I'll happily talk to you, but 1 don't feel at home in your language. Please interview me in English.'

Andrew Clayton, Editor, Business Daily*, Channel 4*

If someone knew English, French and German then they should be well covered for anyone who might want to talk to them.

4

THE TELEVISION INTERVIEW

The Studio Interview

To a stranger [television studios] are frightening places, encapsulating everyone with a sound-proofed blanket – not a whisper, no faint grumbling of distant traffic, no clock ticking or birds singing. There are no windows, there is no natural light: once inside a television studio you cannot tell the time of day, or even the time of year. You are suspended in a small completely artificial box, somewhere deep in space ... studio guests are expected to be overawed ... if you make an effort not to be, it will help you and make the studio crew respect you.

TV & Radio – Everybody's Soapbox[1]

The studio is a hot, scaringly bright jungle of cables, cameras and technicians. The atmosphere is brisk, terse and preoccupied. And the nearer you get to transmission, the more the perspiration and adrenalin will flow – and not only yours.

Getting There

A large TV company may have several studios, so before you set out for your interview, make sure you know *which* to turn up at – and *who* to ask for when you arrive. Take care to anticipate the rush hour and traffic difficulties and aim to arrive early, with enough time to spare to ask someone to show you around the studio. If they can this will de-mystify the place and make it less intimidating.

If transport is a problem, or if you'd prefer, the television station will often agree to send a taxi to call for you. If it would help you to arrive unflustered, take it. And if you have to come under your own steam, you'd be well advised to get someone else to drive you.

Hospitality – Beware!

Nerves can loosen the tongue, especially backstage in the green room where hospitality is handed out. Bite your lip. Be cautious about nervous chatter that might give away too much about your subject beforehand, even if you do feel a desperate need of a friendly face to confide in.

Only say in the green room what you're prepared to say *on the record* in the interview, or you might find yourself facing a loaded question or comment during the actual interview. Remember, your interviewer is on the side of his audience, not you, and he may try to get you to reveal your own hand:

> I understand the deal stretched your finances considerably possibly even took you to the brink of bankruptcy?

or:

> On the face of it your case looked pretty watertight, but at the public inquiry you were sweating – why?

Even if you manage to wriggle out of it without giving an out-and-out denial which could later be exposed as a lie, the shadow of a doubt would be cast. Your best bet is to keep your own counsel.

If you followed the pre-interview checklist earlier you will already know who you'll be appearing with. If it's a rival, chosen to balance the argument by putting the opposing point of view, the same applies: *careless talk costs lives.* Avoid arguing your case with him/her in hospitality – save your ammunition for the real battle.

For refreshments, stick with cool, clear water or black, unsweetened coffee. Avoid sweet milky drinks, which can clog the palate and gum you up. Only drink alcohol if you would die without it, and then make it one *short* short at most to calm the nerves – you need a clear mind and a sharp set of wits, not an aura of false self-confidence. You're better off taking to the bottle when you're safely home after the interview. Avoid beer which is gassy.

If you're nervous that's good. It's when you go in brimming with confidence that you need to worry. Adrenalin is for fight or for flight. Too much and you will want to cut and run. Too little and you won't know what hit you. Just enough and you'll make a good fight of it.

If you're feeling particularly tense, relax yourself by taking a deep breath and stretching. Hold it in tension for a few moments before letting go. Make sure you do that *before* you face the cameras! And if you can't get away from the crowd, take a tip from newsreader Andrew Gardner:

> As you approach the studio door, the palms get sweatier, the mouth gets drier and all those carefully rehearsed phrases vanish. The mind goes blank!... Try this; fill your lungs fully and then let the air out slowly a couple of times about a minute before the interview is due to begin. No one will notice and it works wonders. I know, because I've been doing it for years![2]

Just Checking...

There are a few things you need to be sure of before the interview begins: that the interviewer is who you were expecting; co-interviewees are the same and the ground to be covered hasn't shifted. If the area of questioning differs wildly from what you were led to expect and would leave you at a serious disadvantage, protest. In an emergency, refuse to go on air – unless you would be content to stride on to a rugby pitch dressed in cricket whites. Ask for an idea of the first question in particular, because it's this that will set the tone for the entire interview. Find out how you'll be introduced. Ask to see the cue, which sets the scene and reveals the angle the interviewer is taking:

> Industry now, and the Japanese are after yet another slice of our heavy manufacturing. Welsh Steel, it seems, have been

made an offer they just can't refuse, and shares are soaring in anticipation of the successful takeover by the Japanese conglomerate Kisho. The main shareholder of Welsh Steel is its chairman, Ivor Thomas. Mr Thomas, 15,000 jobs are at stake – are you going to take the money and run, and is this going to be another sell out to the Japs?

Forewarned is to be forearmed, and if you've done your homework, a little bombshell like that one shouldn't be unexpected.

I want to know how am I going to be introduced, and after I'm over, how are you going to sign me off? They could say, 'Here's Mr Benn, one of the most dangerous revolutionaries in British politics who is now about to give us one of his familiar outbursts. '
    The 'health warning' is very important because it is a way in which the interviewer can indicate how the listener should react to what he or she is about to hear.

Tony Benn

Check whether a taped report is to be screened before or after the interview, and ask for details of both what is said and who is saying it. (As we said earlier, preview is a privilege, not a right, but you can but ask...) And you *must* know the length of the interview.

Setting Up

Very little will be explained to you as you enter the studio. You'll be led to your seat by the producer or floor manager and introduced to the interviewer. Studio lights are startlingly bright – and hot. The lights will be on you and they can be dazzling, so try to avoid looking directly into them. If you find yourself wanting to screw up your eyes against them, don't – unless you want to look like a camel with constipation. Fight the temptation and keep your eyes wide open and relaxed.
    Next someone will clip a microphone to your lapel, tie or dress and fuss about running the cable beneath your jacket or around your clothing. It's a bit like being fitted up by a tailor, so don't worry about it. Just let them get on with it and be careful not to brush the

mike once it's on you. Should they forget to provide you with a glass of water, ask for one. Nerves can dry the throat faster than a sandstorm.

Sound Check

In a moment you'll be asked to give a sound check. Speak for 20 seconds or so, leaning slightly forwards as you would during the interview. Look at the interviewer and talk as you intend to during the interview, with the same amount of volume and projection.

They almost always ask you what you had for breakfast. Keep on describing some mythical gargantuan feast until they tell you to stop (this is an opportunity to break the ice, so be as bizarre as you like!), and then keep your position and avoid bellowing or whispering once the interview proper begins.

Be *very* careful what you say anywhere near a microphone. Even if the programme has yet to start the mikes will probably be live, and you never know who might be listening! Every word uttered in the studio can be heard in the control room or gallery where the director sits. Vital advice is to never swear in the vicinity of a microphone – whatever the provocation – pass only obsequious comments about other people, and if you're the US President, avoid wisecracks during the soundcheck about annihilating the Soviet Union – for one thing, times have changed:

> My fellow Americans, I am pleased to tell you we have signed legislation that would outlaw Russia forever. We begin bombing in five minutes.
>
> Ronald Reagan[3]

For another, you can never be sure when the tapes are rolling...

Floor Manager

During the interview, the floor manager's task will be to relay the director's instructions in sign language. This variation of flagless semaphore will be aimed not at you, but at the interviewer, who will have to interpret his signals and act accordingly. When the interview

77

is about to begin, the floor manager will give a countdown. This will probably begin verbally and end with a show of fingers, so that you'll be in no doubt as to when battle commences.

Babel!

TV studios can be distracting places, but the presenter has the biggest distraction of all. He or she has to wear an earpiece. Listening into this is like eavesdropping on the tower of Babel. It pipes into his or her ear the sounds of everything going on in the control room, where the director and team are labouring like rocket scientists at mission control to put the programme out on air.

Among the crowd will be someone with a stopwatch, timing the items, editors advising on cuts and delays, the director instructing the videotape operators to run their machines. The presenter will hear it all. The idea is to pick up any instructions intended for them, and to catch the first warning sign of any problems that are looming.

So if your interviewer appears at any time to be a little distracted, that's because they are! And never more so than towards the end of the interview, when he/she is glancing up at the floor manager to catch signals, listening to instructions about which camera to turn to next, and already beginning to think about the item that is to follow. Everyone else in the studio will also be wearing headphones and listening to the control room, so don't expect to be the centre of attention! Remember, you are talking through the interviewer to your audience, so press on regardless.

TV news studios can be places of barely restrained chaos. You can never expect anybody to tell you exactly what's going to happen, or even necessarily exactly what time your interview will take place. In a news programme, priorities can be turned upside down by a major breaking story like a political resignation or a terrorist bomb. Your interview might be delayed. It might even be dropped. News items can change, programme running orders can alter, sometimes at a moment's notice. So if your interview is delayed or cut short, don't bother protesting, just put it down to the unpredictability of news.

The Remote Studio

Most TV stations operate small outposts known as remote studios. Inside is a single TV camera, operated by remote control. You've seen the result on TV: the interviewer in London or the regions turns from the guest in the studio and addresses an uncomfortable looking individual pictured fiddling with his earpiece. If the distant guest has been well-briefed, the two will appear to be looking at one another through the television screen, but the apparent eye contact is all an illusion.

You won't see your interviewer in the studio, except perhaps on a monitor to one side of you which will show the picture being transmitted. The director will tell you beforehand which way to look; either at the camera or the monitor. Do exactly as he says. If you look to the wrong side of the camera the interviewer and yourself will be facing the same direction, and the result will look as though you're both deep in conversation with a third party who never appears on the screen!

If you are asked to look at the camera, simply pretend its unblinking lens is the face of your interviewer. Act and react as though you really *do* have eye contact, and respond with the appropriate facial expressions. Without a real face in front of you, you may have to work at coming over with some warmth. No problem. Just watch the birdie and *smile*.

And remember, even when you're not being spoken to, the camera will still be trained upon you and your picture may be up on the screen, so keep up the facade of eye contact throughout. You'll be given an earpiece so you can hear the interviewer's questions. These can be uncomfortable. The presenter's de-luxe version has been moulded to fit *his/her* ear. Not so yours. The earpiece and trailing wire look untidy, so if you're to be turned to one side, you'll need to wear it in the ear that's away from the camera. The wire will run behind you and be hidden beneath your jacket or clothing.

Without being able to see the expression on your interviewer's face it's possible to misunderstand the meaning of what he/she is saying, or the purpose of the question he/she is asking. The arch of an eyebrow or sudden switch to a frown will have gone unnoticed,

And another problem is you won't know when the interview is about to come to an end. That means it's more difficult to go for the big payoff, and you're more likely to be interrupted by the interviewer saying, 'Thanks, but that's all we've got time for.' Generally, remote interviews require an element of play-acting and greater concentration.

Location Interviews

Television is a slave to pictures. The more visual a story and more dramatic the pictures, the more prominently it is likely to feature in a news bulletin or programme. Sometimes perfectly valid news items are run well down the bulletin or even dropped because of the absence of good pictures to go with them. At other times, a curious chequerboard of real news and no-news is assembled, where meaningful words are dropped in as fillers among picture stories with little meaning at all.

Conversely, the strength of TV news is that it not only tells people what is happening, it takes them there and shows them; so basic to the news judgement of the TV producer is the need for strong, colourful, exciting pictures. That means interviewing on location.

For a location recording the producer is looking for as much movement, interest, variety and atmosphere as possible. Sometimes he or she may simply want to interview you in your home to ring the changes from yet another uninspiring studio-bound interview. What they are looking for are shots that sum up you or your business. The producer's priority is atmosphere, yours is to show yourself and your company to your best advantage, so be selective about where you allow the cameras to go.

Good light levels are required, so indoor shots will often be near a window offering natural light. Within those constraints, prepare in advance a backdrop that would offer the best image in every sense. If they want to film at your office or plant, make sure the place is tidied up beforehand. Remove anything that might undermine the effect, such as pin-up calendars. If the crew insist on picking their own locations, send a polite and helpful minder around with them to discreetly steer them away from problem areas.

If you're on home ground, try to seat yourself behind a desk since it adds authority. If the TV crew take half an hour to set up, don't sit there getting nervous. Go and have a coffee.

Chartered accountant Paul Turner[4]

If the shoot is to be in your office, show them a desk that's clear enough to convey efficiency, but not so empty as to suggest inactivity! And try to make sure that the company name is in vision, by placing a suitable calendar or notice in a strategic position on or behind your desk.

Studies in the United States have shown that, where there are books in the background, the interviewee comes over as sensible, respected, and authoritative.

Denis MacShane, *Using the Media*[5]

One useful tip: if the location interview is to be out of doors, have some hairspray handy!

Pre-chat

To prepare the ground, the reporter will usually discuss the interview with you in what is known as the pre-chat. This is your chance to clarify the line he intends to take and to steer the interview away from trouble. You may also take the opportunity to introduce some information that the reporter might not have considered, or to suggest a line of questioning he or she might have missed. But in the end, the reporter will exercise the editorial freedom to pursue whichever line of questioning he chooses, without announcing that to you first.

The best interviews are where chemistry flows between the interviewer and interviewee and both are performing well. It's in the reporter's interest for you to give your best performance, so there's often a certain amount of collusion before the start of the interview.

If the interview is purely informational and there are no conflicts of interest the reporter may save editing time by discussing the possible questions with you and going over your likely answers. Some are happy to be blatant about it:

81

What I need is ninety seconds, so I will ask you these four
questions, and your reply will be something like this... yes?

Rob McKenzie, *Broadcast Journalism*

Don't be offended, the reporter is acting as your unpaid producer,
and you are in the fortunate position of being able to choose whether
to take his/her advice.

The important thing is to say at the beginning, 'Look, if I get it
wrong, can I stop?'
No matter how experienced you are, you sometimes find
yourself waffling on, and you know you're not making good
sense... simply stop in the middle and say, 'Look, that's no
good; let me start again.'
At the end of the day, most interviewers want a decent
interview as well, and they're happy to do that.

Des Wilson

Shooting the Location Report

The crew

A typical crew would include a camera operator, sound recordist and
possibly a lighting electrician. On occasions, you might face a full-
blown documentary crew including director, assistant and
technicians.
The crew and reporter will usually travel separately. Once they've
wrapped up this story, they may have to part company to cover
different assignments. That means they may arrive on location at
different times. Sometimes the lighting electrician may also turn up
on his own, so be prepared to welcome the crew in dribs and drabs,
and for them sometimes to be uncertain about exactly what they're
doing. This is because the reporter is often the only one who's been
fully briefed.
Make the crew at home and try to win their affection. If the crew
take a dislike to an interviewee, they can turn even a cover girl into a
pasty-faced cadaver. Coffee, biscuits and somewhere to sit while

they wait for the reporter to show up and the offer again when they have finished is the best way to keep them happy – that, and the opportunity to set up and get on without interruption immediately. The crew might have a number of assignments to cover, and would plan to spend no more than an hour in your company, however congenial you may make it.

The crew need to know *precisely* where they have to go for the interview. That room must not be a place where other things are going on at the same time as they're trying to set up. It's sensible to set up in an available meeting room and then the man can come out of his office, sit straight down and do the interview there.

Andrew Clayton

The shots

Most recorded interviews are conducted with a single camera. The camera operator will shoot pictures of you first, then move round to take shots of the reporter asking questions and reacting to what you say. When these shots have been edited together, they'll give the impression of one continuous interview. The additional shots will also be used as glue to join the sections together. This process may seem strange at the time.

For a location shoot the reporter will want to take general views.

These are scene-setters, such as the exterior of your plant or the interior of your office. Then they will take an establishing shot, or an over-the-shoulder two-shot which they will use to begin the interview. This will show the two of you talking; what you say is not important. The camera will probably remain in the same place for the interview, but will zoom in on you, so the reporter will then be out of vision.

After the interview, the camera may switch positions to get shots of the reporter reacting to your answers. This produces the bizarre spectacle of your interviewer talking to thin air, or stranger still, nodding, smiling, frowning, concentrating or raising a single eyebrow as though listening intently to your conversation.

These cutaways or reaction shots are used to cover the edits in the interview. During the interview the camera is trained on you all the time. That means that when the editor comes to join together two separate shots, there's bound to be a jump, because you'll have shifted slightly in your chair between those shots. They could get away with editing the soundtrack and you'd never notice the join, but the pictures would show you leaping around in your chair. So to join your two sentences together, a cutaway or reaction shot is used to cover up the jump in the picture.

The edited report will show you finishing your first point. Then it'll cut to the reporter listening as you start to make the second point they've selected, before cutting back to you. Other insert shots may also be taken. These are to illustrate the report and, once again, to cover up the edits. You may be seen dialling the telephone, then speaking into it, or they may want to show you addressing a client in your office. Beware of shots of the hands. These can reveal stress, nervousness or tension. Make clear, positive gestures or keep your hands still.

To avoid embarrassment, reporters often prefer to wait until the interviewee is out of the way before taking cutaway shots. At some point the reporter will probably record some of his questions again to camera. If you stay you can check whether the repeat questions are the same as the ones he actually asked – or whether they've been embellished.

Reporters will sometimes tidy up their questions, rephrase them to summarise a point, or put them in a better way to sharpen their style and appear more professional. Nothing wrong with that – just make sure the rephrased questions don't show you up in a bad light:

First question: So what do you stand to gain by holding off a settlement?

Well, the longer we wait, the more we'll save. Every day, we save £50,000 on the wage bill, but of course, the real point is that we can't *afford* to settle. It's impossible to meet their demands without going under. And the longer this drags on, the more business we stand to lose.

Revised question: Now, you stand to save a small fortune on the wages bill by holding off this settlement. But, of course, no production means no income for the company, so isn't this a drastic and damaging way of saving money?

The reporter is less likely to rephrase his questions in a hostile way with you present.

Make Your Own Recording

Make a point of recording the interview yourself. Set a cassette recorder on the desk, out of vision of the camera, but in sight of the interviewer, and without your having to say a word, he or she will know that a record has been made of *what* has been said, and *how* it has been said; which can concentrate the mind wonderfully should there be any attempt to simplify or alter the meaning during editing.

When will it go out?

When it comes to finding out when the edited report is to be transmitted, be prepared for a non-committal answer. The reporter is probably not being evasive – the scheduling of the item is down to the programme editor and the dictates of news. And nobody can predict exactly what stories might break between recording your interview and the transmission of the programme. Midday news summaries will frequently begin with no clear running order and only a handful of finished items. If it sounds like a nightmare, it can be:

'On Tuesday it was a quarter past five and we had 31 seconds for the entire programme. Everything else was still being edited.'
'What do you take for the ulcer?'
'Vodka – and lots of it.'
From the Newsroom of BBC Ulster

If your item doesn't have a fixed sell-by date, it may be kept in reserve or held over for another day. Ask for a copy – most won't but some will, and some charge. And news people are unlikely to remember to phone you to let you know when your piece is due to go out. Your best bet is to phone the producer to check and then record successive editions of the programme until you eventually get it. The problem is less acute with current affairs and programmes using longer items which are usually less prone to the vagaries and disruptions of news.

Actuality Interviews

You've seen those programmes: people at work, rest and play letting it all hang out while the camera crew, sound recordist and attendant paraphernalia tramp round on tiptoe and hide under tables doing their level best to be inconspicuous.

This is *cinema verité*, or actuality, where the illusion given is that you in the audience are there, watching it unfold before your very eyes, without the reporter muscling in as mediator and intruder. It's fun, but of course, it's a fake.

Your llama farm in the Surrey suburbs, staffed by a co-operative of Bolivian *émigrés* and left-wing poets has, for some reason, attracted media attention.

Slice of life programmes are unlikely to give you a hard time.

Except perhaps when it comes to the interview, because the reporter's voice is absent from the recording. That means the viewer is denied the benefit of hearing his questions. So you will have to answer in statements:

Not: Mr Albert Simms, tell me about your llama farm, which you've been running for the past two years here in Esher. What persuaded you to do it?

But: Look, what I want to know is how you came to set up this llama farm, so you'll need to begin by saying something like, 'We set up this llama farm in Esher two years ago – just me, Bolivar and Jean-Paul- because, etc.' OK?

If the camera is trying to capture a slice of life, ignore it – but forget it at your peril. *They* want to show you warts and all, but *you* still have to present a picture that does you credit. They'll tell you to act naturally. So act naturally – carefully.

Masterclass

Des Wilson, General Election Campaign Director, Liberal Democrats

The most important single rule in dealing with television is to understand that there is no law that gives them rights over you. People get frightened of it, but you need to lay down your own laws and say, 'No, I won't be interviewed standing by a motorway, I will be interviewed sitting at my desk. I will not crouch in a peculiar position because it makes the picture look better. I will do it my way.'

You'd be amazed at how *mad* that makes television people. They'll say to me, 'I want you to walk in here and do this and that,' and I'll say, 'Sorry, I don't feel right doing it, so I won't do it.'

And they think you're a prima donna or unreasonable. The ability to intimidate is considerable, and to make people feel, 'Oh well, I should cooperate', but you've got to have the strength to say, 'No, that's not right, that doesn't work.'

I'll give you an example. For the fifteenth anniversary of Shelter [the Housing charity] I went back and did a tour around the country with its current director. The idea was first director and current director go back and look at bad housing together. A lot of the interest was in me coming back, but it was essential that he get *his* share of the publicity, because he was having to go on to do the job. So we agreed to do the programme jointly.

We got to one place and the interviewer was extremely rude and arrogant and said, 'Look, I've come to interview Des Wilson, I'm not interested in you. If you want the story on air tonight, stop buggering me around and let me get on with interviewing Des Wilson.'

And I just said to the chap, 'I'm sorry, but we don't want the publicity *that* much that we're going to let you distort what we're trying to do here.' I called his bluff. And he said, 'OK, then I'll interview you both,' and he did and it went out and it was fine.

You must remember this: once a crew has come out, they need *you* as much as you need them. That guy doesn't want to go back and say to his producer, 'I'm sorry, I had a row with the guy and I've not got the interview.' His job is to get it, so you're in a position of some power to control the situation.

Tony Benn, MP

Record the interview if it's important. I've learnt this over many years and I have found it *immensely* helpful, because I can type up and compare the uncut and the edited versions. Put them together and you can then detect with a red pencil where the cosmetic surgery has been done.

I have actually recorded everything since 1974 so I have got probably five or six thousand hours of speeches. The only time I have used it absolutely contemporaneously, is when I feel they have mis-edited it.

I remember on one occasion I was asked a question when I was a minister about a strike at London Airport, and I began by saying, 'Well look, I'm not the Minister for Employment, you will have to ask him, but looking more generally...' and so on.

And the BBC put it on as, 'Commenting on the strike at London Airport, Mr Benn said...' Then a Tory MP put down a question asking the Prime Minister whether the statement made by the Secretary of State for Energy about the strike at London Airport represented the policy of the Government. The Prime Minister wrote to me asking, 'What did you say?'

So I was then able to type out what I had said on the interview *and* the broadcast and show with the red pencil how the trick had been performed, that they'd put a different answer to the question. That got me off the hook, but also it was a very useful check.

People keep copies of letters, but they don't keep what they have said. And of course what they *say* is bound to reach a larger audience and have more effect.

It's fine by me if, like Tony Benn, they want to tape-record the interview themselves. The more the merrier. The whole game is to get people to say things, not make them up.

Lynn Barber, *The Independent on Sunday*[6]

5

THE RADIO INTERVIEW

My own experience suggests that radio is a critical influencing factor on both the perceptions of a local MP from within his area and thus on eventual electoral chances.

The beauty of the radio medium is its greater capacity for news, its swifter turnaround of material and its lack of mechanical baggage in the setting up of a story.

Question Time in the House [of Commons] ... is the best opportunity for the backbencher to catch the Speaker's eye and inject a comment. That done you need only stroll a few paces across the lobby to a nearby telephone and dial the local radio station. Nine times out of ten they'll want audio for the next available news bulletin on the hour. The least you can usually bargain for is a line of copy. The exchange need not be historic, merely local and relevant. And, thanks to the wonders of interviewing down the telephone line, the story is immediate. You hang up... secure in the knowledge that your name, and probably your voice, is going out across your area over the course of the afternoon... Not something to be sniffed at, I assure you.

Charles Kennedy, Liberal Democrat MP[1]

Radio news looks for similar things to TV – the short, pithy, quotable quote or the three minute interview. But being grilled for radio is usually less of an ordeal than the spit-roasting you may receive on TV. Radio is usually faster, friendlier, simpler, more accessible and often more fun. It is also smaller, cheaper, leaner and fitter than TV. The chain of communication is very much shorter with fewer bodies falling over one another in the production process.

Radio in the UK is cut three ways, between the BBC and the Independent stations, the local and the national, the speech-based and the music-based, and the medium is expanding. The appetite for news is insatiable.

One of several things could happen. After a call to set things up a reporter could come out to you and record an interview in your office, or you could be invited to go into a studio. There you might be asked to record an interview, be interviewed live or take part in a live discussion programme, much like television. Or you might be telephoned and asked to record a short interview there and then for use on a radio news bulletin. These are called *phonos*.

Come what may, your pre-interview procedure is similar. In brief: check out the context – what the item is about and what angle they're pursuing. Do they want you to go live, or to record you? Find out what kind of report it's for. Will it be used as a short, stand-alone comment in a news bulletin, or will yours be one voice among several in a longer item – if so, who else is on the piece and what are they saying? Find out when the item is to go out and how long the final piece and your contribution to it is likely to run.

If your radio interview is to be live, prime a colleague to make a recording from a radio cassette recorder, so you can listen back to your performance later. Have the facts ready, because most radio newsrooms move at such a pace that the news reporter is often inadequately briefed. He/she knows what kind of comment or reaction they want, but can sometimes be less clear about the facts of the story.

Local radio and newspapers tend to value their contacts more highly than the national media. They will want to use you again in the future, so they will be less inclined to screw you up and throw you away the first time.

> Local radio, just as local newspapers, has an overt interest in maintaining good relations and needs to keep them bubbling along.
>
> Alison Sergeant

The interview, providing the subject is uncontroversial, will be a simple exchange of information – more of a collaboration than a clash of the titans. But even in commercial radio, news and advertising do not mix so waving your account over a journalist is unlikely to make him keep his head down.

The Recorded Interview

Radio news deadlines come crashing down every hour, on the hour. If you are being approached to give an interview for a radio news bulletin, the reporter will need to record that interview *immediately*, and to hasten back with it forthwith. Forget the complementary drinks, guided tours and other pleasantries.

The reporter's aim will often be to get the piece on the next available bulletin, which means life has to be lived at a sprint. Unlike colleagues in TV, the radio reporter functions without a cortege. Instead of camera operator, sound engineer, lighting technician *and* a journalist, you'll have just one hassled individual and a tape recorder to contend with.

Setting-up

While a TV electrician may scowl at the gloom in your office and turn up enough blinding wattage to fry an egg, in radio, sound is everything. The radio reporter is likely to frown and tell you your office echoes like a bathroom, your air conditioning is clamorous, your phone is a threat and your windows will have to be shut. It's even possible that your lights will have to go off to eliminate a buzz from the recording.

If the acoustics are too bright they'll produce an echo which *you* won't realise is there, but the microphone will pick up and amplify. This is produced by the sound rattling around the hard surfaces. Most rooms will produce an echo, unless flat surfaces are amply broken up by drapes and plenty of soft furnishings. Even then, most living rooms will reverberate like vaults, and the average office can resemble the changing room at a rugby club.

If there are any distractions, real or potential, the reporter will demand an end to them. He/she will want you to silence your secretary, your phone, fax and anything else that swishes, hums, whistles and is likely to pipe up while the recording is in progress. As a last resort they may suggest drawing your curtains to try to dampen the sound. Comply, even if it means handing over hush money to your staff afterwards! If that fails they will probably ask to shift you to another location. The ideal interview room is somewhere small and cosy with soft furnishings. In desperation, do the interview out of doors.

At one businessmans' conference ... the late Sir John Methven, as CBI Director General, found himself being interviewed for radio in the ladies' rest room. It was quiet, and as it happened, the radio reporter in question was a Ms... Nevertheless, prior planning would have prevented the problem arising.
The headline business, CBI/Abbey Life

However good your office, the radio reporter will not want to record an interview with you behind your desk. One difference between radio and television is the type of microphone that's used. The radio reporter will have a hand-held mike which will work most effectively some 35 cm from your mouth. To get it to your mouth and back to theirs in time for the next question, the reporter will have no option but to sidle up to conduct the interview. This is in contrast to television, which normally points a gun mike at you from enough distance to keep it out of vision.

The radio reporter will have to get much, much closer. Closer, in fact, than is usual in polite company. In body language terms, your personal space will have to be invaded. Normally that only happens when you are fighting or flirting. So if it is your first time on radio be prepared to feel a little *hormonal* about the close proximity required.

The radio reporter will need to winkle you out from behind the desk, if he/she is to avoid stretching across the top of it to record you. Besides, the desk's flat surface would produce its own echo for the microphone. So either you will have to come out or they will need to bring a chair round to join you. So be prepared for the office furniture to be rearranged and the semiotics of authority along with it.

The ideal recording position is knee to knee. The reporter will sit either facing you offset with their right knee close to your own, so he/she is able to hold the microphone correctly without having to stretch, or at 90 degrees to you. Don't be intimidated by the microphone, which can look a bit like a balled fist in front of your face and make you want to recoil from it. If the radio reporter knows how to use it they will tuck it away, beneath your chin and out of sight, so it ceases to pose a threat. If they fail to do that, the secret is to look past the microphone, fix the reporter in the eyes and keep smiling.

If all that is wanted is a comment for a news bulletin, the reporter will want from you little more than 20 to 40 seconds of useable material – at the standard three words per second that's 60 to 120 words. The interview is likely to continue for a little longer, but the surplus will end up on the cutting room floor, as 20 seconds or so is the length of a clip or sound bite used to illustrate a news item. Experienced radio reporters won't waste their time. They know the more they record, the more they will have to edit. They will tell you what's required, discuss the angle with you and let you know precisely what is needed from you. If they know you're experienced, they may ask you the one major question, and you should be able to answer it succinctly to time.

Radio stations differ in their requirements. Those which place a greater emphasis on music than speech will often prefer shorter durations – especially pop stations that go for pace and punch. With a major story of some complexity, the reporter may want to take several different clips covering different angles to allow the station to ring the changes in successive news bulletins (see also the Sound Bite). Bearing in mind that your comments are likely to be chopped up into bite sized chunks, even if the interview is for an item of several minutes in duration, make sure everything you say has a positive angle to it. Keep your sentences short, simple and declarative and let each make *one* clear point.

The radio reporter's brief may be to record a longer item, often for the peak-audience breakfast show. The typical BBC local radio breakfast programme is a blend of speech and music, with the emphasis on speech. And the kind of material they are looking for could be a straight interview of up to three minutes in duration, occasionally less, or what is known as a *package*, a short report, featuring a number of different voices.

If you are to appear in a package, then the amount they will use of you will depend on the number of players involved. If the package is three minutes long, then they may want less than a minute with you, run as a single clip, or in segments across the item. Follow the same rules as for the television interview and you will be fine.

You can be working on three or four major stories a day with little research backup. You go in and do your three and a half minute interview, pick out your 20 seconds of actuality, do a voice piece, and at the end of the day, you've got to say, well, actually, I've just skimmed over a number of issues.
    Richard Bestik, former IRN Parliamentary Correspondent[2]

Sound Effects

As TV thrives on pictures, so a lively radio report requires interesting sounds to evoke images in the imagination of its audience. If the reporter is producing a package, their interest in the sound will extend beyond the concern to eliminate intrusive background noises and extraneous echoes, to searching out sounds which will illustrate the report. What are wanted are sounds that depict the subject in question. If you are in a factory the reporter will want to record the machinery in action. If you are launching a new product the first thing they will ask you is, 'Does it make any noise?' These are radio's pictures: sirens screaming, presses pounding, even phones ringing and being answered – anything that paints a clear picture in the imagination. Providing the noises are not too intrusive, the reporter may wish to conduct the interview with those sounds in the background. Or they may wish to record them separately and mix them in later as background noise beneath the interview to give it atmosphere. Background sound effects are known as *wildtrack*. Most radio reporters will be suitably impressed if you can point them in the direction of good ambient sound or wildtrack.

The Phono

Some radio stations which have only a small newsroom with limited staff can't afford the time to send their people out to gather interviews. So they may call you and ask you to record an interview down the telephone. This is called a *phono*.

The trouble with phonos is that by the time they are recorded, re-recorded for editing, re-recorded again for playback and transmitted on the crackly AM frequency and pumped out through the three inch speaker of a transistor radio the audibility is analagous to mumbling into a sock at someone with their hands over their ears. It's even worse if you happen to be listening on the average car radio. Phonos make unattractive listening. Drivers may be tempted to turn over or turn off. Even on the clearest line your voice will sound reedy and thin, because telephones cut off all bass and treble leaving a mid-range mush. So sometimes the reporter will call you back until you find a clear line.

Thanks to their immediacy phone interviews tend to be used for short, instant items for radio news bulletins. Pressure will be on for you to record an interview *immediately*. Few reporters will expect to be told that you will call them back. But don't be stampeded. Only go on air right away if you are absolutely confident about what you intend to say. As ever, play for a little time, check out their area of questioning and arrange to call them back in ten minutes when you have had time to plan your response. But don't leave it any later, or they may switch resources to some other story and you will have missed the opportunity. Remember, radio may be working to hourly deadlines.

It is unlikely that anyone would record an interview with you and use it on air without your permission. This would be against all guidelines, and a justifiably serious cause for complaint. They should always ask you if they can record an interview and tell you *when* they are recording it.

If you've agreed to give the interview, they may insist on calling you back, so they can do so from a studio equipped to record phone calls. So their voice can be recorded in studio quality, rather than on a tinny phone-line, they will then try to route your call through a mixing desk. I said *try*, because it's amazing how often you simply vanish without trace in the plumbing.

When they succeed in retrieving you, they will take a level check to balance the volume of your two voices. Sometimes it can be difficult to get sufficient volume from a telephone. If they have trouble hearing you, either speak more closely into the handset or a little louder. Never bellow unless you want to sound like a maniac.

If the reporter is still unhappy with the levels, they will redial and start again. If you are being asked to go live into a programme, make sure your own radio is turned off to prevent the howling sound produced by feedback.

Because radio news is a slave to speed and the reporter is rushing to beat the deadline by doing things the quickest way possible, they may seek a little more collusion than is usual. It's in their interest to save time on editing. An experienced interviewee will be able to produce a perfectly timed bulletin clip which needs no editing. Find out how long they want: 20, 30, 35 seconds, and make your response to suit. The reporter will almost always edit out their questions, so it is better if you give one good answer, using the familiar system of points and pointers we described earlier.

If you have established sufficient rapport with the reporter and have enough confidence in your material, you could begin by finding out exactly what they want to ask you, and start your reply with a measured countdown: 'Three, two, one...' before launching into your precisely timed reply. It is the technique the radio journalist uses for recording voice reports (where there is no accompanying interview) and is a great help when it comes to getting material on air quickly. After a while you can get to be a dab hand with this, and radio reporters are more likely to come to you for interviews. You understand the game that they're playing, and you are succeeding by playing it by their rules – which is what promotion through the media is all about. Eventually, you might even receive the ultimate accolade – the dubious title of 'Rent-a-Quote'.

The Radio Studio

Short of a reporter turning up on your doorstep or bending your ear on the telephone, you may be asked to go along to the radio studio to either pre-record an interview or go live into a programme. Compared with television, radio stations are often low-tech and impoverished. Few at a local level will be prepared to lay on a car for you or even pay your expenses for coming in. Local radio sees itself as serving the community. You have some bearing on the community, so they are asking you to come in at your own expense as part of *your* service to the community. It's worth it. It builds up good relations with the media and your constituents, clients and power-brokers in the audience. And the sound of you talking to them in their kitchens is far more personal than any number of flat black words on the page of a newspaper. But before you agree to go, check *which* programme you will be appearing on and who will be interviewing you so you can get an idea of what is in store. If you are unfamiliar with the programme, ask the producer to describe it to you, and if you have the luxury of time before making your decision, listen to a show or ask the producer to send you a tape.

The radio studio is a total contrast to its television equivalent. It's usually small, cluttered and dark. If you are giving an interview for a news programme, you may be interviewed in a newsbooth, which is tiny, cluttered and dark. Your interview will be recorded on a reel-to-reel machine and later edited for transmission.

If your host is a music presenter, then he or she is likely to know even less about the issue than a jobbing journalist. Their brief and the questions they will ask will probably have been provided by the producer. So make sure you talk to the producer about the direction of the interview and ask to see the introductory material. During the interview the producer will sit in an adjoining room behind glass where he/she can maintain eye contact with the presenter and verbal contact via headphones. He/she will direct the course of the interview.

If your studio interview is to be live your host will often be in the driving seat operating the mixing desk himself with its mission-control array of buttons and switches. What follows may be rather like trying to engage the captain of a plane in conversation during take-off.

Your host will be working all the faders, carts, grams, tapes, CD's and phone equipment, cuing-up forthcoming records and commercials, bending an ear to the producer and will still be expected to sound informed about the subject and interested in what you have to say... Often they will resort to firing questions from the producer's list, and while you are answering, will then busy themselves preparing whatever tape or disc comes next. Half the time, you could reel off lines from Shakespeare and they wouldn't realise. They are just waiting for you to pause so the next question can be fired. There is usually little to fear, but to do the job, a presenter has to be sharp, and you could cut yourself badly on the best of them. Self-operated programmes such as these are barely disguised bedlam and that is the way they like it. These people live on a diet of caffeine pills. The day they bring out adrenalin drops you won't hear them for crunching.

In the UK, self-ops are more prevalent in the commercial sector, where cost-cutting is rife, than in the BBC. The ideal situation is where the interviewer is relieved of technical considerations by a studio manager and can be free to attend to the interview. If the subject of the interview is particularly newsworthy, it will probably be recorded so clips can be taken for later use in news bulletins, or the newsroom may want to interview you separately afterwards. It is worth checking.

Phone-ins

Most radio stations also have a *talks studio*, which is a room with a single table, often octagonal with several microphones branching from its centre. This is used for round the table discussions and sometimes for phone-ins. You might be invited to be a panel guest on a radio phone-in, giving callers the benefit of your expertise in answer to their questions. Phone-ins can be a little more disconcerting than live interviews, because neither you nor your host can predict what the caller may ask or say. Prepare well for all contingencies. Never let yourself be pressed into appearing immediately on a *live* discussion programme. It is unreasonable not to be given time to think and to prepare.

To fend off cranks who slip past the producer most radio stations operate a form of censorship known as a delay system. This works by broadcasting the programme several seconds or so after it has actually taken place, giving the presenter a breathing space in which to hit the panic button.

Microphone Discipline

In television you are wired up with a lapel microphone. In radio, you tend to sit at a desk with a microphone pointing at you. Don't be put off by it. Look beyond it and attempt to gain eye contact with the interviewer. Make sure that you lean forward to position your face no further than 50 cm from the microphone (a short arm's length), and no closer than 15 cm (a hand's length).

Be sure you are sitting comfortably for the level check, because you mustn't shift from that position as it would upset the sound balance. Also take care if you are using notes that your bundle of papers doesn't brush against either the microphone or its stand. This is all-too easily done and makes a horrendous noise. Ideally use A5 rather than A4 paper for brief notes or better still a filecard. Card or firm paper is preferable, as it can't flop over and drag across the table making a noise close to the mike. But remember, even though your notes won't be seen, you still *mustn't read from them.*

Similarly, many microphones are mounted on stands which go through the centre of the desk. Be careful that you don't accidentally stretch your legs out and kick it. If you do, it will reverberate all the way up to the microphone. If you have just come in off the street and you are still in your overcoat you may be asked to remove it if it is made of material which is inclined to rustle, because with the microphone so close it could sound like fire breaking out.

At the same time, expect the producer to ask you to remove jangly bracelets which might clatter and to rebuke you sternly if you start thumping the desk or clicking away at the top of your biro. The mike will amplify your thumps into thunder. You might be asked to wear headphones. Too loud and you can be drowned out by your own voice. Ask them to adjust the volume until it is comfortable. Every studio has its red light. When that's on – so are you. Any idle conversation has to cease mid-breath as soon as that light flickers on.

The Remote Studio

Presenter: 'Mr Banham?'

Mr Banham: 'Yes?'

Presenter: 'Are you on the line?'

Mr Banham: 'Well, of course I'm on the line!'

Today, Radio 4[3]

The radio station remote studio is similar to its counterpart in TV, but there isn't even a monitor to look at. Remote studios are usually in places such as county hall, with the aim of persuading politicians to step out of their committee meetings and pass comment – not difficult. The studio is often little more than a cubby hole with headphones, microphone and a sound mixer, and a county information officer hovering around to slap your wrist if you press the wrong buttons. Not the most congenial of surroundings in which to conduct an interview.

Interviewees feel isolated. They don't know the context in which this is taking place as well as they would if they were in the studio taking part. The questions come out of the ether. They can't see the interviewer and so don't always appreciate the *way* in which the question is asked. Without that eye contact, you can't see the beginning of a smile, or the seriousness of their expression, or tell when the interview is coming to an end. They can't read the signals, so it can be very offputting for an interviewee almost to be told in the middle of a sentence to shut up.

Despite that some people actually *prefer* to be interviewed that way. They prefer to be isolated and concentrate only on the questions and not have the distraction of the studio and the strange environment, with mikes, desks and all the frenetic activity.

Bud Evans

The Radio Car

You know you're a celebrity – and so do your neighbours -- when instead of calling you in, they agree to send the radio car out to you. The neighbours can't miss it – it's usually a big shooting-brake smothered with radio stickers and dominated by a vast, dangerous-looking antenna. All the comments about the remote studio apply, except the radio car is doubly cramped and the engineer is even less likely to press a cup of tea on you before putting you on air.

The purpose of the radio car is not primarily to save celebrities the cab fare to the radio station, but to have a facility available to permit live broadcasting from the location of a breaking story, such as a serious fire.

Some seasoned interviewers are getting wise to the fact that the BBC is prepared to send out a radio car for them and that they don't always have to turn up at the studios. But don't ask for the radio car if you are being called on to take part in a live discussion. Sitting there in splendid isolation you won't be able to catch the eye of the presenter when you want to chip in and nor will you be able to see what the other guests are up to.

Bud Evans

Your Voice

On radio, as with television, you need to be bright, lively, positive and confident and seek to establish a rapport. But one significant difference is that your audience can't see your face, so an important element of your communication is lost. To make up for it, you will need to channel all your expression into your voice – without sounding like a Shakespearean actor!

Radio favours rich fruity voices and is unimpressed by those which sound thin, reedy, piping or lightweight. To be frank, it doesn't much care for women's voices unless they have the richness of Eartha Kitt. And that's got a lot to do with the distortions caused by the tinny transistor radio. As Dina Ross writes in *Surviving the Media Jungle*: 'I have to deliberately lower my own naturally high-pitched voice or I sound like an intoxicated Munchkin.'

If you try to *change* your voice, you do so at the peril of losing your naturalness. But you can make the most of what you've got, by thinking deep, opening your throat and making your mouth, lungs and larynx *work*. But don't try it for the first time on air – practice into a tape recorder. More on how you present your message later.

A Happy Medium

Radio's easier than television. You can sit down with an *aide-memoire* of the points that you want to get across. And after the first couple of sentences you almost forget you are on the radio.

John Pike

Radio is an altogether friendlier place to learn the art of media communication, and the techniques of the interview are similar to that of television. So, if you get the opportunity to cut your teeth on local radio, be inclined to take it. Local radio identifies with and affirms its audience and the area in which they live, so if you are *for* the listeners, the station will be for you.

It is worth getting to know both the news editor and the programme controller or programme organiser on your local station. Most radio stations have a division between news and general programming. Make sure you promote yourself on both sides of the radio station. Never expect them to pass on anything to one another, they seldom do.

Broadcasters who've had experience of both radio and television will tell you that television, with its constant distractions to the eye is a much less satisfactory medium, for those who have something to say and know how to say it.

Ludovic Kennedy

Masterclass

Alison Sergeant, News Editor, BBC Radio Cambridgeshire

It's amazing how many people come along and think they are going to be interviewed about one thing and in fact are interviewed about something completely different, because of a communication breakdown.

It is certainly worth running through with whoever greets you on arrival to look at the introduction material to find out if they have got your name right. I know it's the reporter's job to check these things, but curiously enough, if you start to correct them on air, you lose the sympathy of the audience because there's a curious relationship between the audience and the presenter on local radio. They tend to *own* their local radio presenter. They care about him; they'd say, 'Oh, he's telling our John off, that's not fair!' So they won't be on your side if you do on-air corrections, so run through that with the reporter or presenter on arrival.

WHAT HAPPENS IF THERE'S A CLASH WITH THE BUSINESS COMMUNITY?

Local radio needs to maintain good contacts with local companies. It happens all the time, particularly with crime stories, that the national press will tread heavily over a situation and beat people into submission and then go away again, because they don't care about future good relations. But we can't afford to break the rules and we have to play it by the book by being fair and reasonable to people.

That doesn't mean I won't challenge people, if there are questions that should be asked, I will ask them fairly, but I will give people a fair hearing and will end up with a balanced report.

DO THE NEWSMAKERS REALLY RECOGNISE THE POTENTIAL OF RADIO?

I'm sure many don't. They don't tend to appreciate either how *local* radio effectively acts as the BBC's news gathering service in whichever region they are working.

A story might start off with a phone call to Radio Cambridgeshire. That same story will be handled by one of our reporters who might pass it on the Radio 4's *Today* programme. It might find a slot on *Outlook* on the World Service, or one of the science programmes. It might be to *Woman's Hour, You and Yours, Does He take Sugar* – any number of network programmes are hungry for material from local radio.

Equally, it can lead them to regional television because we work very closely. It's only a phone call away from regional television. We are in liaison several times a day with colleagues from regional television. We tell them about stories which will make nice pictures, because we have, as do many local radio stations, a small television unit working from our offices.

They also work in very close liaison with network television, so it might be the Nine o'clock news or John Craven's *Newsround.* That's how it works.

6

NEWSPAPER AND MAGAZINE INTERVIEWS

It is quite astounding that a simple interview where one individual, whatever his position, perhaps in intemperate language, expressed what so many are thinking, should have created such a storm.

Letter to *The Spectator*, following the resignation of British Industry Secretary, Nicholas Ridley

A Technology-free Zone

Newspaper and magazine interviews are not the unarmed combat they once were. Reporters have taken increasingly to plonking a cassette recorder on the table in front of you. It leaves them free to concentrate on asking you questions without having the twin worries of getting it down in shorthand and wondering whether they'll ever be able to read it back again. In any event, never underestimate the firepower of the low-tech spiral bound notebook.

An in-depth feature for a newspaper or magazine will obviously require a longer interview than for a short news item on the electronic media. Deadlines are less immediate than radio, so the pace may be more civilised and the surroundings, released from the worry of light and sound levels, can afford to be more convivial. But lunch appointments are likely to be the exception. The majority of interview requests will be for a straightforward quote or two to follow up your news release, and they will often be conducted over the phone.

You often get a much better interview face to face, but the phone is quick and doesn't involve either party travelling.
    Executives are busy people and often think interviews will take much longer than they do. They often misjudge the value of spending two or three minutes even on the phone with a reporter. In that time you can answer a *lot* of questions.

John Bryant

Be mindful of press deadlines, and if you are dealing with a magazine, remember that the publication date may be several months away, so what you say will have to be appropriate then. Deadlines and lead times vary, so check before you prepare your message or lay on a three hour lunch.

Time makes me graceless. 'How was your journey?' asks the polite interviewee. 'Fine,' I say, slapping down my tape-recorder and getting out my list of questions. Once Julie Andrews was telling me about her children and asked, 'Have you got children?' 'No,' I said, abolishing two daughters without a second's thought – good heavens, she might start asking me their names and ages, and whole *minutes* could be wasted.

Lynn Barber[1]

Before agreeing to give the interview, the usual checks apply. Find out who is doing it and what length they intend it to run. And ask whether it's for a news item or a feature article. Features place a greater emphasis on the human interest angle, and that may mean passing comment about you.
    Getting the name of the interviewer is even more important, because if you are dealing with a specialist you will need to know where they are coming from politically. Journalists working for UK newspapers and magazines, unlike their colleagues in broadcasting, have no obligation to be impartial in their reporting. They can be as loaded as they like and emerge from anywhere in the political spectrum. Their only worry is the law of libel. So whether you run a

union, a pressure group or a company, it pays you to be familiar with their journal and, if possible, with your interviewer's track record.

If you are being interviewed by a specialist reporter, such as an industrial or political correspondent, then you can expect your interrogator to be rather better clued-up on the subject than a news reporter from radio and TV. A radio reporter may spend twenty minutes with you, but for a standard package, he is unlikely to use more than a minute and half – that's 270 words. But a magazine feature can run to a thousand words or more. To get that they may want to see you for up to an hour.

In a longer interview it's just as vital to get your key points across, and to avoid diluting them by including excess material which they may decide to print instead. Your two or three key points and supporting pointers should contain enough material to allow you to talk on that subject for 20 minutes or so. That's 3,600 words. Twenty minutes might not sound long, but if what you say is pointed and pertinent, you would have said enough to fill not one, but *three* feature articles. If you do run out, don't fog the issue by bringing up new points, simply amplify the old and offer additional supporting material, such as appropriate anecdotes or analogies.

Dangers of Distortion

Even stripped of the trappings of technology, the newspaper interview is no more a conversation than is the confessional. It too, has its formality and its ritual. An accomplished interviewer will be conspicuous by his silence. He/she will listen attentively, and occasionally offer the briefest of interjections, such as 'Why?' or 'How?' Clever questions might bolster the image of a presenter on the box, but in print it is only your *answers* that matter.

Be wary if the newspaper interview is the other way round; if he/she does most of the talking and you just nod. What is published could be little more than your tacit endorsement of someone else's opinion. Conversely, the more you say, the more scope there is for him to be selective with your words. In radio and television where they are using actuality – your actual quotes – it's what they throw away that can distort what's left in. But in print your words may be boiled down into reported speech, where the reporter is summing up what he/she *thinks* you have said. Their rendition of your account will be a summary, and thereby a simplification.

After the interview, there is little point in asking a journalist to show you the written-up copy before it goes to press. To do so is to say two things: you don't trust the reporter to get it right, and you want the power of veto over his/her material. Neither will get a warm reaction. If new facts come to light which render what you have said inaccurate or irrelevant, then call the journalist immediately. But bear in mind that once the paper has gone to press, it will be too late to make changes, and any disruption will be unwelcome.

Don't be Seduced...

What you say will be taken down and used in evidence against you. So think before you speak. Treat the news reporter like a colleague who's after your job. You *have* to be congenial, you have to work together, but you have to stay on your guard and be wary, unlike the government minister in the case study on p. 113.

Of every breed of reporter, it is the print journalist who bears cheerfully the reputation of being a beer-sodden hack. Of course that's an *exaggeration*... The same rules for drink apply. Don't. Too many people have said 'yes' as a result of alcohol and woken to regret it the following morning.

Because the print journalist's news-gathering apparatus may be no more obtrusive than his attention, you can never be sure when a reporter is actually interviewing you. Beware of friendly chats, or a drink and a word at the bar. Treat every meeting with a reporter as an on-the-record interview. It is far easier to let something slip with a print journalist than when a camera or tape recorder is trained on you. Remember Watergate!

Strong Arm Tactics

Local papers, like local radio, are looking for good news stories about the area. They like to say 'This is a good place to live, good things are happening here.' They will value you as a contact and so are less likely to give you a hard time than their hit and run

109

colleagues on the national press. It would take a serious story to make them put the boot in.

In the main, they are likely to be supportive of you – especially if they rely on your advertising. But, as with commercial radio, if you do have a substantial account with the paper, don't be lulled into a false sense of security. On most paid-for papers, editorial and advertising accounts are separate and the news staff resent and will sometimes strongly resist attempts from the advertising department to soften a story or prevent them from running it. They'll fight for their editorial independence. So if a bad news story breaks your hefty account may offer little or no leverage. Plough your nervous energy into preparing a superb interview.

Press Pictures

> Satisfaction with his latest trek (to Britain, Denmark and Iceland) does not overcome a certain caution. Confronted by a camera, the South African President sweeps the glass from the table and places it at his feet. 'I don't think we should have this in.' Photographs taken, the whisky-and-soda is sipped appreciatively between drags on his John Rolfe cigarettes.
>
> Stephen Glover and Cal McCrystal, *The Independent on Sunday*[2]

Similar rules apply to the press photo as to the TV location shoot. If the feature is a study of you, a head and shoulders shot in your office against some books may do, but if it is more to do with your business, then have in mind some locations that will offer pictures that are both interesting and evocative and show your workplace off to its best advantage.

For shots of yourself the photographer will either pose you or just snap away while you are being interviewed. *Beware the candid camera.* Photographers usually go for the point of action. For a subject as static as a head and shoulders, that could mean something as subtle as a widening of the eyes or a smile. If you pull faces or make expansive gestures they are guaranteed to take them, not always to good effect. The picture may be used against you at some later date:

Margaret Thatcher is looking strained and upset. Her eyes are tightly closed and her left hand is against her face, covering one eye. 'It was a question about Rhodesia that caused her to put her hand over her face – and I've never caught her doing it since. The picture always seems to be used when she is in trouble'.

Sally Soames, photographer, *Sunday Times*[3]

Ask beforehand for the right of veto of all negatives or only agree to give posed shots, or have your own shots taken.

It can be useful to have a portfolio of current, ready-made, shots on offer, which you can caption later to suit the situation. But the media is looking for something more than shots of grinning blue-suits standing shoulder to shoulder. *Pictures matter.* A good shot will span several columns and draw the eye to it. And the bigger the picture, the more space will have to be set aside for the accompanying write up, even if they only use a caption. And as anyone who's ever worked in newsprint knows, pictures sell papers.

The following advice from the Business Editor of a Birmingham paper holds good whether you are preparing your own portfolio, organising a shot for a news release or planning for the visit of a press photographer:

We'll always publish a decent picture with a bad story, just for the sake of the picture. It might not be a big story, but if it's a decent picture, we'll use it.

We are looking for something a bit more dynamic, that's got some action to it; something with a good backdrop.

A very good shot we had recently was of a company that makes big pipelines 15 feet across. All the people were standing inside the pipeline. The sun was shining in from behind and it lit up this group of people and looked very dramatic.

Others have been people standing on the twentieth floor, with the backdrop of the city behind them; people standing on spiral staircases – arty shots with a little ingenuity.

111

Always have people in your shots if you can; especially on something like a digger or piece of equipment. Having a person standing near it gives the machinery some perspective.

Russell Hotten

Graphics

While television may be reluctant to run your graphics, because your artwork is unlikely to conform to their station style; less style-conscious local newspapers will often be grateful. Russell Hotten again:

Graphics are very useful. Newspapers are using them more and more. They help the designers layout the pages and they break up the text. They look good, and obviously they're informative.

Reporters shy away from packing stories with facts and figures. Even with financial stories, the more figures, the more turgid the article becomes and the less likely the reader is to plough through it.

If a reporter can avoid using too many facts and figures that's ideal. The reader can get the bare bones from the story and if they want the details, it's in the graphic.

And there are two reasons why graphics can work for *you*: like a photo, a good graphic could make the difference between a piece being used or being dropped; and if it *is* used, you have only yourself to blame if your figures are presented inaccurately.

If you can show on a pie chart that 60 per cent of the price of a gallon of petrol is tax, then that probably means much more to people than a percentage symbol.

John Pike

Masterclass

A Little Gaffe about the Germans

I never dreamed as we went to press that she would ask him to resign because of this interview.

So wrote Dominic Lawson, editor of *The Spectator* as the UK Industry Secretary, Nicholas Ridley, ruefully took his leave from the Government front benches after making a few choice comments in his magazine about Britain's European cousins.

Mr Ridley exemplified the British Island mentality and perhaps the private views of his Prime Minister, when he allegedly dismissed plans for a joint European monetary policy in the following un-Ministerial terms:

This is all a German racket designed to take over Europe. It has to be thwarted. This rushed take-over by the Germans on the worst possible basis, with the French behaving like poodles to the Germans, is absolutely intolerable.[4]

Still digging himself in furiously with a stout shovel (made in Sheffield, no doubt) he reportedly then dismissed the European Commissioners, Britain's among them, as 'seventeen unelected, reject politicians'. Then, in the next breath, he said of Chancellor Kohl:

He'll soon be coming here and trying to say that this is what we should do... I mean, he'll soon be trying to take over *everything...*

And in a defiant eulogy of the British bulldog spirit, continued:

...you don't understand the British people if you don't understand this... They can be dared; they can be moved. But being bossed by a German – it would cause absolute mayhem in this country, and rightly, I think.

Was he misquoted? Had an off-the-record confidence been abused? Apparently not. 'All the quotes came from a two-hour recorded interview agreed – almost a month in advance – to be entirely on the record,' insisted Dominic Lawson. Furthermore: 'None of the remarks I quoted are prefaced or followed by the phrase, "this is not for quotation", which appears two or three times on the tape.'[5]

Ah, then the minister must have been *tired* and *emotional,* surely? After all, the interview had been preceded by lunch. But no, it seems not:

> The rumbustious tone of Mr Ridley's remarks and the fact that our conversation was post-prandial may give the misleading impression that the politician was relaxing and not choosing his words too carefully. Far from it. Mr Ridley had the smallest glass of wine with his lunch, and then answered all my questions with a fierce frown of concentration.

So if Mr Ridley was quoted right and had not been bent on committing political *hari kiri*, it could only be that he, and Dominic Lawson both, for some reason, failed to comprehend the effect the offending words would have.

In his resignation letter, Mr Ridley said he believed his views had been 'very much in line with those of the Government. But I recognise the difficulties which my failure to use more measured words have caused.' Hindsight has a brilliant, if merciless, quality; but as a commodity, it is never there when you need it. But why did neither Mr Ridley nor Mr Lawson have the foresight to recognise the potential impact of this public expression of opinion held privately within the Government?

'You may be a good journalist to get the story,' grinned Kelvin MacKenzie of the *Sun*, Britain's most widely read newspaper. 'But not good enough to realise just what a story you had.' And to make the point, he 'took up' the interview (read: filched it) and spread it across the centre pages of his newspaper. Given such a splash, the Minister's indiscretions couldn't fail to be picked up by the rest of the media – at home and abroad.

What was taken to be the central theme of the interview was distilled and conveyed with even greater impact by the accompanying cartoon in *The Spectator*, which was reproduced on the continent. It portrayed Mr Ridley as a vandal on the run, paintbrush in hand, fresh from daubing a tell-tale toothbrush moustache on a poster picture of Chancellor Kohl.

The *Frankfurter Allgemeine Zeitung* was not amused. Taking its cue from the cartoon it sniffily declaimed Mr Ridley as a 'Europa-Hooligan'. And *Le Monde*, miffed at its countrymen being compared to an obsequious poodle, observed starchily that Mr Ridley was somewhat less than a gentleman. Duelling being so passé, and with the UK's reputation as *enfant terrible* of Europe buttressed yet further, Mr Ridley's resignation became inevitable.

As the dust cleared, commentator Paul Johnson pondered aloud in *The Spectator* :

> Why do ministers give press interviews. What is in it for them? Why not do the natural thing for a politician, and make a speech instead, or even write an article?... Speeches are... vetted, commented on by advisors, reconsidered.

Mr Johnson suggested that if the minister really was determined to risk his all with the media, then he should have had one of his own officials present to cough discreetly over his master's indiscretions, and even then he ought to have insisted on the right of veto over the article's contents:

> The only real safeguard is for the minister to insist, as a condition for granting the interview, on a written guarantee that the text, as it is to be published, be shown to him, and an opportunity afforded to make changes. Journalists hate having such terms imposed on them as they wish to keep in any headline-catching indiscretion which may come their way. But that is precisely why the minister should insist. Had Ridley done so, he would still be Her Majesty's Secretary of State today.

But the real crime for which Mr Ridley was hanged was one which he did not commit – quite.

The damaging cartoon comparing Chancellor Kohl with Hitler was the magazine's invention. The simile was clearly in the mind of its editor, who suggests rightly or wrongly that he read it first in the mind of Mr Ridley. But what actually came

115

from Mr Ridley's *mouth* was the observation that if Britain were to surrender sovereignty to the European Commissioners she might just as well have handed sovereignty over to Hitler 50 years previously. The bending of the equation to produce the fatal identification between Chancellor Kohl and the Führer was made explicit not by Mr Ridley, but by Dominic Lawson in his own running commentary:

> **Lawson:** 'But surely Herr Kohl is preferable to Herr Hitler. He's not going to bomb us, after all.'

> **Ridley:** 'I'm not sure I wouldn't rather have...'

> **Lawson:** – I thought for one giddy moment, as Mr Ridley paused to stub out his *nth* cigarette, that he would mention the name of the last Chancellor of a united Germany –

> **Ridley:** ' – er... the shelters and the chance to fight back, than simply being taken over by... *economics*.'

Rash words. But it was the combination of a cartoon and that comment that ensured his downfall. As Paul Johnson observed: 'One of the golden rules of public utterances is never compare anyone or anything to Hitler.' He could usefully have added: and never give the media the chance to make the connection for you.

Mr Ridley might not have said it all, but he clearly said too much.

Most damning of all was that he expressed what his superiors were embarrassed to be caught thinking. The following week this letter appeared in *The Spectator.*

> Sir: Please, please interview Mrs Thatcher forthwith.
> And bill me for the glass of wine.
>
> Cheryl Brigg

But Mr Lawson had no need. Mrs Thatcher's own hostility to Europe did the job every bit as effectively as any number of articles in *The Spectator.* (See also Foreign Language Interviews p.67.)

> *Moral:* 'Don't mention the war.'
>
> Basil Fawlty

7

PUTTING YOURSELF ACROSS

See how Chris Patten [does] the doggy-wag during interviews.
Note how {Nigel] Lawson relies on the eyes-front hammer
nod, combined with shoulder dip and hip swing. Observe the
Hattersley horizontal jowl-judder. Michael Meacher's pulpit
projection, Geoffrey Howe's slight levitation at moments of
emphasis as though he has springs in his heels or ants in his
pants.
        And you ask yourself, from which of these would you buy
a life of assurances?

Hugh Hebert, *The Guardian*[1]

They say 80 per cent of people make up their minds about
somebody on television within the first 30 seconds. But I'd say
90 per cent and 10 seconds.

Media consultant Diana Mather

How You Look

'Cut to camera two...' And you're on. In the space of a smile the
audience will decide whether they're for you or against you. They'll
weigh you up and make their choice, sometimes even before you
open your mouth – just like at a job interview, really. The camera
will show you in close-up and under closer scrutiny for longer than
even your most intimate friend would care to linger. A sobering
thought! The camera is an unblinking magnifying glass. Fortunately
it's not a very high definition one – yet. But you are advised to take
particular care over your appearance.

Be smart. TV is a medium of images. Cultivate the right image to represent your organisation and yourself. Avoid eccentricity. You should dress to look *confident, credible* and *authoritative.* That means pitching your sartorial sense somewhere between a wedding and a funeral; neither too showy nor severe.

For Channel 4's Jon Snow interview [Labour's John] Smith seemed to be perched on an uncomfortable bar stool, which would have been fine had he not chosen to clench his hands across his genitals.

The wearing of a trendy, flowered tie was inspired, and it was a relief to see that the suit strained only a little on fastening.

Sarah Dickinson, *The Sunday Correspondent*[2]

Ralph Waldo Emerson wrote, 'A man's style is his mind's voice.' Your clothes and personal appearance send powerful messages. Make sure they are the messages you want to send.

Milo O. Frank[3]

TV cameras can be distorting mirrors. They don't work exactly like the human eye and there are some patterns and colours they can't handle.

Avoid stripy shirts and very white clothes. White shirts are probably alright under a jacket. Very small check patterns tend to strobe a bit, but it's not as bad as it used to be. Tolerances art: much greater.

Andrew Clayton

Your best bet is a plain, or finely striped suit in a dark but positive colour like navy. Brown will often come over as murky. Black and white can affect the colour balance, and bold, bright colours can appear to bleed on screen. Check with the producer when you arrange the interview.

To keep your suit line neat, carry nothing in your pockets, and if your jacket is long and likely to ride up your back when you're seated, sit on its tail. Women are advised not to show bare arms, or to wear off-the-shoulder dresses – in close up it can look as though you have nothing on. You want your audience to listen to what you're saying, not spend their time wondering...

If you wear a tie, make sure it complements your shirt. Check the knot is tight and central in your collar. The camera will have this in view throughout, so take care to keep your top button covered. Avoid bright metal jewellery which could reflect the studio lights, large earrings which could draw attention from your face, and lapel badges whose message will be lost on the screen and will only distract the audience.

Keep your hair neat. Carry a pocket mirror and a comb and smooth out any straggly ends which the camera and the studio back lighting will exaggerate. Hair should be brushed away from your eyebrows. Your eyebrows convey a great deal of expression. If they're hidden beneath a mop of hair you'll handicap your ability to communicate. Another thing that could hide your eyes is photochromatic glasses, which may darken under the lights.

Some women suffer from neck flushes under stress. These can give away more than your face might suggest. If you're in any doubt, wear a high neckline or a scarf. Use light make-up, where appropriate. If someone offers to powder you down before you go on air, submit. If you think you need it, ask for it. TV puts you under very close scrutiny. Generally they'll use just a light dusting powder to keep your face from shining. If your complexion is sallow or blemished – we might as well be frank about it – then consider getting lightly made up before you arrive at the studio. In the end, it'll be up to you to make sure you're shown off in the best possible light.

Coming into a studio people do need just a bit of make-up to take the shine off – a little powder and foundation, that's all, sometimes not even that – and their hair tidied up.

Some have refused, but when you show them the shot and they see how shiny their forehead looks, they understand that a little make-up is no bad thing.

If the interview's being shot in their office with a mobile Betacam, which is what most people use now, they'll look fine without make-up.

Andrew Clayton

119

Don't smoke. You'll either look seedy or emerge as a fire-breathing dragon. Finally, before it's time to go into the studio, go to the loo and, while you're there, give your appearance one last going-over.

> She [Margaret Thatcher] does not necessarily show her feelings in her face, because she is such a fine performer. She shows them in her hair. Now, her hair is always *done*. There was a time when I could tell how she was feeling by the state of her hair-do.
>
> Sally Soames, *Sunday Times*[4]

> The theory is that if you are on television you wear a new suit and have your hair cut. I think you've got to look respectable, but this idea that if you haven't got a good argument a new suit will see you through is a complete illusion.
>
> If the Prime Minister appeared with an earring through his nose, it might distract you... but sartorial appearance is much overdone.
>
> Tony Benn, MP

How You Seem

Self-projection

> Television... does funny things with your normal, often unconscious ways of communicating. Raising of the eyebrows can make it look as though you are clowning around. A reflective pause comes over as an evasive search for a sneaky answer. 'Ums' and 'ers' which we use all the time in normal conversation become infuriating distractions. Unobtrusive shadows under the eyes are converted into cadaverous hollows.
>
> *Promoting Yourself on Television and Radio*[5]

The television interview is a performance pretending to be a conversation. Even the News is intended to make entertaining viewing. TV is larger than life, and requires a degree of self-projection, that will require you to summon your verve, animation and energy if you are to appear as vital and alert. That said, TV is not the theatre, and your voice and your personality don't need pumping up to the point where they could fill a hall. Take care also to avoid appearing hyper: colleagues will start asking pointed questions about artificial stimulants.

Television is supposedly a naturalistic medium... until you stop to think about how unnatural the whole process is and how far removed from normal life, which seems to somehow keep burbling along without the attentions of a producer. Television's historic role has been to educate, inform and entertain, but in the battle for the ratings entertainment values now reign supreme. There are times when the packaging seems to triumph over content, and that shift towards style over substance inevitably rubs off on news values. So your interview will need to make entertaining viewing. That doesn't mean you should sound like a chat show host... you'll be riveting enough if you are lively and speak our language and tell us in a compelling manner about things of interest which concern us. Add to those virtues sincerity and enthusiasm and you'll be home and dry.

Your audience will turn you off and the TV station will strike your from its contacts book if you are the opposite: wooden, dull, self-important, jargon-laden, uninspiring and irrelevant. You should aim for confidence, credibility and warmth. If you are warm, your audience will warm to you. This can be hard to cultivate when you're under stress, but if people want to look at a cold fish, they'll buy an aquarium.

There are two extremes to avoid – pomposity and trying too hard to please. The audience will not warm to a figure who exudes arrogance; nor will they respect someone who is sweetness and smiles and falling over backwards to please. Avoid any suggestion of insincerity or vanity – be modest, but never unassuming.

Beware of reflecting the mood of your interviewer. An instinctive desire to please can make one unconsciously pick up the other person's signals and reflect them back. Not a good move, if your host is feeling dour, lacklustre or sceptical. Be confident and project your own persona. That in turn will give you greater control and could send the process into reverse, to put a little sparkle back into your uninspiring interviewer.

If you yourself are naturally dry, then to sparkle may involve a conscious decision to be animated. Put some expression into your face. Project your humanity, and not just your ideas. Few would suggest that it was Ronald Reagan's intellectual acumen that made him one of America's most popular presidents. President Gorbachev's acclaim world-wide, if not at home, was down to his personal charm as much as his policies, and a publicity machine that took its cue from the US and made as much of the man as what he stood for.

Despite all appearances from the other side of the camera, TV is a form of one-to-one communication. You're a guest in somebody's front room, so avoid oratario – don't lecture your audience, *speak* to them; and never regard them as an assembled mass *out there*. The best broadcasters will tell you that the secret of communication is to establish rapport and that is done by picturing yourself speaking to just *one* person. The art has come a long way:

Sir Oswald Mosley Discusses Unemployment with British Movietone Gazette (1930)

Deferential interviewer: 'Are you going to talk about unemployment today?'

Mosley [posturing with one hand on his hip, clasping the lapel of his jacket with the other; chest out; chin in the air; voice booming]: 'Why of course! It is the one problem that really matters today.

'This is a period in which politicians are not very popular.

And believe me, you have my sympathies. Politicians are regarded as people who have learned to talk, but not to *act*, and YOU [clutching both lapels and thrusting them towards the camera] DEMAND action ... in dealing with unemployment.'

Are you Sitting Comfortably...?

All head touching is a sign of tension, of course, but the Americans go further. They say every time you touch your mouth, it means you're lying... that's nonsense of course.

Jeannie France-Hayhurst, Corporate Charisma

1 well remember Miss Tipple, my kindergarten teacher, thrusting her ruler against our backs to see how *straight* we sat. Of us all, a little girl with bunches called Susan was the one destined for military service... Miss Tipple would have a thing or two to say about appearing on TV:

'I said, sit *comfortably*, Andrew, 1 did *not* tell you to *slouch*. Put your bottom *back* in the chair, *right* back, that's it. Now lean *slightly* forward... *not* bolt upright! That's better: relaxed, but always smart; ever alert, that's the ticket! Now *where* did 1 leave my ruler...'

Miss Tipple would also have at you for fidgeting or shifting around in your seat, so find a comfortable position and stick to it. If you slide around the camera will have to shift to follow you. When the camera has you in close up there's little room for movement before your face slides out of the frame, so keep reasonably still.

Avoid touching your face, biting your nails, stroking your hair, repeatedly licking your lips or clicking your pen. These are all nervous displacement habits you may not even be aware of. The camera will exaggerate all these commonplace twitches and give them undue emphasis. So instead of fidgeting, which distracts and cuts across your message, use gestures to reinforce what you say.

Normal, expressive hand movements are perfectly acceptable, but expansive gestures should be left to the eccentric scientists. If you can't keep your hands under control without coercion just clasp them lightly in your lap or to one side. Whatever you do, fight the urge to cross your arms. It's almost as defensive as turning your back. Besides, you're likely to bash the microphone. However, crossing your legs is probably a good move, providing you keep them that way, especially if your skirt ends anywhere above the knees.

No-one really knows what they'll look like on television until they've tried it and seen a tape of themselves in action. It's surprising what the camera brings out – it's not always a nasty shock, but the camera has not a single ounce of tact or compassion! The best way to prepare is to rehearse the interview before a video camera and study the tape. It can be a salutary experience and you'll discover habits that you never even knew about! Get some training in front of a video camera before you perform for real.

Adrenalin runs high for everyone in the TV studio, but act confident and you will be confident – you may even enjoy it!

A relaxed stance, careful use of gesture and short, simple sentences.

Ludovic Kennedy

Eye Contact

Once the studio is live, act as though you are on camera all the time as the director may cut to you before the interview begins. Then try to forget the cameras and the lights, the technicians and the paraphernalia. Just concentrate on your interviewer and maintain eye contact throughout.

If you get uncomfortable looking straight into somebody's eyes – and that can happen very easily – there's a very good technique, which is to find a point roughly in the middle of their nose between their eyebrows, and you can apparently be making perfect eye contact with the person. It's a very good television technique, because if you get embarrassed your eyes start darting round and you look very shifty.

Alison Sergeant

One form of eye contact to be avoided is with your audience. Never stare into the camera. A direct appeal to the public cuts across conventions and will make you seem inexperienced or manipulative.

Eye contact conveys a message of equal importance away from the TV studio, especially at the start of the interview. Successful social contact is prefaced by mutual acknowledgement, then acceptance. We have to like and be liked. Or at least pretend to. And we convey that by seeing, smiling, and shaking hands before getting down to business.

As a lecturer in postgraduate broadcast journalism, I conducted an exercise in interviewing which was videotaped. One of my students, now a rising star in television – he's improved no end – performed what was dearly the worst interview of the session. It was embarrassing to watch. He seemed utterly preoccupied with his portable recorder and his notes. There was not even a token attempt at establishing rapport. During the course of the five minute interview he and his interviewee occupied worlds of their own. There was scarcely a moment when they so much as exchanged a glance.

As a result, precious little information was exchanged either, and the end product was every bit as unfocused and lack-lustre as the social contact between them.

Good eye contact at the start needs to be followed through with good eye contact throughout. It is not only a way of affirming your interest in the other, but a method of taking control.

How You Sound

Do use your voice. Remember that if you *are* enthusiastic about something you can make your voice *sound* enthusiastic about it. You can pace it up or tone it down. If you are concerned, sound it, but without using the classic '*dead baby*' voice, which is the insincere tone of 'I really do care most terribly about everything that has happened' – certain politicians are very good at the dead baby voice. You can sound concerned without sounding theatrical. You can sound measured, you can have oodles of gravitas, or sound jolly and happy. *Use* your voice; it's a very powerful way of selling your message.

Alison Sergeant

The elements of good delivery are pitch, pace, clarity, animation and emphasis. Nerves can literally strangle a voice. If you think yours might be inclined to twitter up an octave or two, sit up with a straight back (where's that ruler...) breathe deeply from the diaphragm, and form your words with not only your lips and your teeth, but your whole mouth. The wider your open your throat the deeper your voice will sound. Also, the harder you work your mouth, the less likely you will be to speak too quickly, as many bright people are inclined to do under pressure. Clarity will also improve as you limber up that jaw.

Next aim to put some sparkle in your voice. *Animate*. Come alive. If you maunder on in a monotone, you can be sure they'll pull the plug on you in your prime. Watch out for verbal ticks like ums and ers, unnecessary pauses and saying 'Well...' at the beginning of each sentence.

Never fake an accent or try to iron out the kinks in your own. You'll never be able to keep it up, and they'll never let you live it down in the office! And one day, when your name is well-known, someone will dust off that archive recording of you with a plum in your mouth... Proclaim your accent with pride. The BBC, for one, is out to promote regional accents, and besides, they add character.

Use emphasis *wisely*. There's nothing more boring than a drone, or more irritating than a tub-thumper who bangs your ears with every fourth syllable. Correct emphasis brings alive the meaning of your sentence. Tryout the following:

We will *take* the appropriate action.

That's what you'd expect to hear. But see how the meaning changes as the emphasis is shifted:

We will take the appropriate action.
(Not *you* – us.)

We *will* take the appropriate action.
(Honestly!)

We will take the *appropriate* action.

(So you know where to put *your* featherbrained suggestion!)

We will take the appropriate *action*.
(Threats?)

We-will-take-the-appropriate-action!
(And that's my last word on the subject!)

Listen to yourself on a cassette recorder. Be honest. How do you sound? Most people loathe their own voices when they first hear a recording of themselves. The most important thing is that what you hear strikes some kind of rapport. It must reach out to you and get your attention without demanding it or wheedling for it.

If you sound flat, follow the advice given to aspirant presenters.

Find a book of children's stories written to be read out loud and let yourself go. Imagine you are presenting *A Book at Bedtime*. Bring them to life. Give all the characters different voices. Enjoy it. Listen back to it with a critical ear; or better still, try it out on a captive audience! A few sessions like this will do wonders for your delivery.

Authority is not a *sound*. Authority is a state of *knowing* what you are talking about and being able to explain it convincingly and readily to somebody else.

David Dunhill, BBC voice trainer[6]

Masterclass

Liz Howell, Managing Editor, Sky News

We would never make-up anybody who was being interviewed outside the studio. Otherwise make-up is very simple; just a sort of dust-down with powder. We don't even bother with foundation, although it depends on their skin, of course. And we don't do a remake on women, just tidy them up. All you want to do is keep the light from shining off them. Years ago you had the odd man who was silly about it, but we don't get that sort of thing now.

Des Wilson, Veteran Activist and Liberal Democrat General Election Campaign Director

I don't think what you say on television matters as much as how you *look*, funnily enough.

By how you look, I don't just mean that your hair's done nicely and you're wearing tidy clothes; what I mean is that you look relaxed and in command and likeable and intelligent. It is an impression you convey; people either instinctively feel confidence in you or they don't.

So when you're interviewed, don't let television people put you in circumstances that don't work for you. You've got to be satisfied that you are going to look good and sound good, otherwise you're put at a disadvantage.

When I was running the lead-free petrol campaign, just in order that they had pictures, television people would take me out and put me beside a motorway, and there I would be shouting to make myself heard over the passing traffic, my hair blowing in all directions.

127

And then you would see the Minister sitting quietly in his office, immaculate. Well, who comes across looking the most reliable and sound person? The guy screaming hysterically by a motorway, or the guy sitting quietly behind his desk?

Don't let them sit you or stand you where you'll feel silly, because if you *feel* silly, you'll look silly. Insist that you sit in your office or your usual chair, and as comfortably as possible. That's important, because if you feel right in the situation, you feel more in command of it.

8

PUTTING YOUR POINT ACROSS

First of all, don't turn up looking like a tramp. Secondly, allow yourself plenty of time. There's nothing worse than arriving hot and sweaty and in a lather, having to rush in and sit down out of breath. Thirdly, answer the questions asked. If you don't you will be seen to be evasive. Fourthly, try to do it as naturally as possible. That means using humour and informality, and conversational gambits, as you would in ordinary conversation.

Jeremy Paxman

Now we come to the crunch. Your suit line is pressed and perfect. Your skin aglow with a dusting of translucent powder. Your message drilled, rehearsed and honed to perfection; a golden thread running through every sentence. Deflector shields are up and phasers are on stun. But can you deliver?

Business people lacking experience of the media reveal their vulnerability in the studio. They spend too long saying too little. They answer direct questions indirectly. Their body language undermines the positive image they are trying to project. They appear not to have anticipated the trickier questions.

'How to go on air and survive,' *The Times*[1]

Communicate

> Good presentation ... is good projection of yourself, not putting on a performance.
>
> Harvey Thomas, former Conservative Party Director of
> Presentation and Promotion

First let's repeat a warning. Never memo rise your material. If you do, unless you are a skilled actor, you will be looking inside your head to read the script when you should be reaching out to your audience to communicate.

Real rapport is only achieved when your energies and attention are focused *outwards* towards your listeners. Any kind of script, inside your head or on paper, becomes a strait-jacket. The effect of conversation is lost and you become stilted and unnatural. Instead, outline your material, know it and rehearse it, but never let your material get between you and the audience. What you are aiming for is spontaneity.

Get to the Point

Get straight on with it. Don't dither around with preliminaries, such as 'Yes, hello; good morning.' If you are in a remote studio and have yet to establish contact with your presenter it may seem polite and proper to say something by way of introduction, but consider how irritating that sounds on radio phone-ins.

If you followed the advice earlier, your argument will have been broken down into sections and those sections placed in order of priority. Brace yourself for the possibility that you may not get the opportunity to state all of your points. If you can give only one, then that point must stand up by itself without support.

You are fighting the clock. You have a limited time to make your case, and that will dictate how you will state the point. Get to the point *immediately*. Don't lead in towards it. This is not like a court case where you begin with evidence and end up with a verdict. State the verdict *first*.

If by some miracle you find time on your hands after stating your points, then reinforce them by finding a different way of saying the same thing. The spoken word is fleeting. For an audience to take in and grasp what you have said, they may have to hear it several times. Don't be afraid of drumming the point home. But be creative in the way you reiterate and state your points.

Be Brief

> You tend to be conversational, whereas you need to be precise. You have a small window of opportunity to make your point and if you're not trained you'll miss it. Keep your hands still, your chin up and look at the interviewer. Make your statement and wait for the next question. Don't waffle.
>
> Joe Forster, Management Consultant[2]

Keep your comments brief. Sentences should be short, simple and declarative. Strive for clarity and conciseness. Leave out anything that will dilute your argument or distract from the main point. State each point and accompanying pointers, and pause in between for comeback. If you aim for answers of 40 seconds or less you will avoid repeating yourself, or defeating yourself by adding spurious qualifications or equivocations.

Don't try to give an interview that is impossible to edit. Some people think that if they pause for breath in the middle of a sentence rather than at the end they won't be able to cut the interview and will be forced instead to run it in its entirety. In practice, rather than attempt to edit the interview, the producer will probably throw it away:

> He was an academic – a sociologist – and every sentence was full of the most horrendously long words. I say sentence, but he didn't really speak in sentences. Just when you thought he was going to come up for breath, he'd plunge into some tortuous phrase with renewed vigour. I did my best, but he was impossible to edit. The man needed *subtitles*. And that's a pity, because he was sincere and what he had to say was significant for South Africa. It needed to be heard, but in the end they couldn't use it.
>
> World Service freelance

Words are like shovels. You can use them to dig yourself out of a hole or dig yourself deeper into one. And the more you dig, the deeper you get. Keep it short, especially if the point is controversial.

Cut and cut until you are down to its essentials and then give them all the impact they need. If you concentrate on one point and put it over, it will make more impact [on TV] than 2,000 words in a newspaper article.

Sir Frederick Catherwood[3]

Be Positive

Be well briefed, know the subject inside out, put it over convincingly, and be positive.

Philip Ditton, CBI

The media idea of good news is usually bad news, and if you've been called in over a bad news story, be sure to press home the positive aspects of it and avoid going on the defensive. Make it your aim to leave the story on an upturn.

Terry Steel, Public Relations Director for Boots, the high street retailer, says managers are briefed to avoid going on the defensive over controversial issues:

We look at interviews as a positive opportunity to talk about what we have done successfully in retailing and manufacturing.[4]

Be definite. Don't be vague. Avoid any sign of equivocation:

I think	I mean to say	maybe
Perhaps	it seems to me	*nice*

Remember, the devil's advocate will have his claws out to probe your weaknesses. Unless you speak with conviction, doubt will be assumed. Project yourself as being decisive. At the same time be careful to avoid stating possibilities as facts and turning shades of grey into black and white. Lack of time and the need to speak in plain English will generate pressure to oversimplify issues, but clarify your points during your preparation – not in the studio.

Gladstone said he had six rules for speaking: simple words, short sentences; distinct diction; testing one's arguments beforehand; knowledge of subject and watching the audience.

Ludovic Kennedy[5]

End With Impact

Your audience will remember the beginning and the end of the interview more clearly than any other part, so having begun well you need to finish strongly with a strong, emphatic, positive and encouraging statement:

So I'm confident that orders *will* pick up; we *will* be able to turn this around, and we *will* move on from strength to strength.

...we may have some way to go, but there *has* been progress, we *are* moving forward, and we intend to build on our success.

We've used the world's resources and we've been grateful. Now we're growing more aware of the needs of the environment, and it's time big business began to put back what it's taken out. We're making a start, and we hope other companies will follow suit.

Live Interviews

One just accepts a very high level of information and confidence and determination, especially if it's live. There is a diminution in the willingness to debate, but that's the media's own responsibility. Because of the immediacy, people are on the record much more. They have had to control, not in the

Orwellian sense, but to make sure that what they say is what they want to say and not inadvertent.

Donald MacCormick, presenter *Special Inquiry* and
Newsnight[6]

Live interviews are over in a flash. You need to put over your main point right at the beginning or as close to the start as possible. The worst thing that can happen is that the interviewer takes you down a blind alley while you're champing at the bit to get over the rest of your message. Quite clearly, you'll need to regain the initiative. In a live interview, success or failure will depend on your sense of timing. If you know when the interview is due to end, you can cut in in the last few seconds and make your point.

Before you went on you would have checked how long the interview was scheduled to run. Now you need to seize the opportunity to cut in. Keep an eye on your wrist watch, preferably held in the palm of your hand. Past master at this is Tony Benn. If a reporter wants 2 minutes 30 that's what he'll give, turning the question to whatever issue he wants, often without pausing long enough for the reporter to get another word in edgeways. The following is only one of many Benn legends, and it appears in Denis MacShane's book, *Using the Media*:

One of television's better performers, Tony Benn, was once asked to be the other guest... on a current-affairs programme. When he arrived, he asked the producer how long the interview would be. The producer said, 'About three or four minutes, we'll see how it goes.' Benn insisted that he wanted to know the exact length... The producer told him that the planned time was in fact 3 minutes 45 seconds.

Benn went into the studio with his watch in the palm of his hand. He took a full part in the discussion. Then, with only 25 seconds to go, he intervened directly into what the other person was saying, with 'Look, what we're all forgetting is...' He spoke until exactly 3 minutes 41 seconds were up, leaving the interviewer with time only to bring the interview to an immediate end.[8]

An alternative is to try to catch a glimpse of the floor manager, and take your cue from him. The floor manager passes on the director's instructions to the interviewer through a series of simple hand signals.

Typically, one finger raised in the air means the interviewer has one minute to go; crossed forearms means thirty seconds; a circular motion of the hand means wind it up – bring the interview to a close as quickly as possible, and a hand drawn sharply across the throat makes its message abundantly clear – cut the interview now!

When the thirty seconds signal comes, you know you have just that time to complete your case, which should always end strongly. The wind-up means that now is the time for the big finish. There's nothing to be gained from blundering on despite these signals. When the cutthroat is shown, your interviewer will *have* to interrupt you and bring it to an end. However you do get your cues, do it discreetly. You don't want the camera to catch you staring wildly round the studio in search of the floor manager.

> The best law of politics, Lloyd George once said, is, 'Don't think about the question they've asked, think about the question that's coming.'
>
> Prime Minister John Major

Recorded Interviews

Live interviews can be nerve-racking, but in many respects they're preferable to pre-recorded ones. With a live interview you have more control of what goes out on air, unless your name is Tony Benn...

> If however, you can't do it live, say to them, 'Well, how much time do you want?' They'll say to you, 'We'll do a fifteen minute interview and we might use three or four minutes,' say to them, 'Well, I'll *give* your three or four minutes.'
>
> Sometimes they've said to me, 'Well, probably it will only be a sound bite [single, short comment], so I've said, 'OK, if it's 20 seconds, I will give you 20 seconds.' And I've learned, and anyone can learn, that if you put a stopwatch on the table, you can speak absolutely to time. There's no particular problem.
>
> Tony Benn, MP

135

Faced with less astute interviewees, more material is usually taped than is needed, and most of it will be discarded, as the reporter selects which of your words he or she wants to use. Obviously, the longer you talk, the more choice you relinquish about what to use, and the less the likelihood of them using the bits *you* thought were most important.

Recorded interviews will seldom – if ever – appear full length on the screen. Most television news items will run for under two minutes, and that will contain the reporter's commentary and a second, third, or even fourth interviewee. Radio features average at around three minutes, depending on the pace set by the music. If you've followed the pre-interview checklist, you will have found out how long the final piece is expected to run, and roughly how long your contribution should be within it. And you will have tailored your response to fit.

Recorded interviews are not always carried out by well-known on-screen reporters. Current affairs teams, producing programmes which go into more depth about the *hows* and *whys* of what's going on than their colleagues in News may send a researcher to interview you, and his or her questions would be cut out later. When it comes to editing a recorded interview, you can help make sure your important points don't end up on the proverbial cutting room floor by flagging them:

The most important issue here is...

Now the main point is this...

Give them an Inch...

Editing to shorten recorded interviews must not distort or misrepresent the known views of the interviewee.
Independent Television Commission, Programme Code

Should you be remiss enough to be unclear in your views, and unfortunate enough to fall prey to an unscrupulous journalist (saints preserve us!) then you could find your words telescoped in such a way that you appear to be saying something altogether different from what you meant. Here's a hypothetical worst case example:

Reporter: Are you in favour of the death penalty?

Interviewee: That's very difficult to say. / YES... / I suppose so, under certain circumstances, but it's an awful thing to take a life, whatever that person has done. When you're dealing with / MURDERERS AND RAPISTS WHO WILL PROBABLY KILL AND RAPE ALL OVER AGAIN AS SOON AS THEY'RE RELEASED... / I don't know, maybe / THEY SHOULD BE EXECUTED. / But there are always those who are genuinely sorry and are serving their time – and while there's life there's hope. They could change. If we take an eye for an eye, all we are doing is stooping to their level. But it's the others, / THE MANIACS AND FANATICS WHO CAN'T STOP THE KILLING – THEY'RE A MENACE TO US ALL. / But that's what prisons are for, isn't it.

Read only the words in capitals, and you will hear a strong, unqualified call for the death penalty. But take the answer as a whole, and that was clearly *not* what the interviewee was saying.

The trouble is that the interviewee said so much, so badly, and is so double-minded that the same words could be edited by the unscrupulous to mean almost anything:

Reporter: Are you in favour of the death penalty?

Interviewee: That's very difficult to say. Yes... I suppose so, under certain circumstances, but / IT'S AN AWFUL THING TO TAKE A LIFE, WHATEVER THAT PERSON HAS DONE. / When you're dealing with murderers and rapists who will probably kill and rape all over again as soon as they're released... I don't know, maybe they should be executed. But THERE ARE AL WAYS THOSE WHO ARE GENUINELY SORRY AND ARE SERVING THEIR TIME – AND WHILE THERE'S LIFE THERE'S HOPE – THEY COULD CHANGE. IF WE TAKE AN EYE FOR AN EYE, ALL WE ARE DOING IS STOOPING TO THEIR LEVEL. / But it's

137

the others, the maniacs and fanatics who can't stop the killing
– they're a menace to us all. But that's what prisons are for,
isn't it.[7]

Controversial issues can't usually be summed up in a sentence. They
need qualification. But be careful – though few journalists would
ride as roughshod over your meaning as in the example, any kind of
'on the other hand' will usually be chopped if space is short – and it
usually is.

The safest insurance policy is, as ever, to *know* what you want to
say and say it clearly, without equivocation, and openly make your
own recording of the interview. It tends to happen less in TV than in
radio or print, because pictures are that much harder to edit.

Editing can sometimes work in your favour. Unless the reporter is
trying to trip you up, it's usually in his/her best interests to edit what
you say to make you sound as clear and as lucid as possible. No
reporter wants to offer an item that's dull and uninspiring.
Sometimes a well-edited interview can make even a poorish speaker
sound lively.

During a recorded interview, if you make a mistake... stop...
pause... recover... and make your point again. That's what reporters
do when they fluff their pieces to camera, so there's no reason why
you shouldn't do it too. Start the whole sentence again, don't try to
pick up on it mid-sentence, otherwise they'll never be able to edit it.

At the conclusion of a recorded interview, be it for television,
radio or print, briefly summarise your main points to fix them firmly
in your interviewer's mind. If the interview has wandered at all, this
is your final chance to refocus the issue.

The Sound Bite

Because of attention span, the average time of all television
news stories is one and a half minutes. The reporter needs 30
seconds to set up the story, another 30 seconds for the
interview or tape of what's happening, then another 30
seconds... to summarize and end the story.

If I go out to interview someone... I want that person to
make his point in 30 seconds or less so I can pull it out and use

it. That 30-second portion... is called a 'sound bite'. If the subject doesn't make his statement in 30 seconds or less, I can't use it and it doesn't make the air.

If you can't say it in 30 seconds, you probably can't say it at all. If you know how, you can make any point very well in 30 seconds.

US TV news anchor, Terry Mayo[8]

The sound bite is the single short comment extracted from an interview which is used to illustrate a news report. It can last from as little as seven seconds to about 40. TV sound bites tend to be shorter than their radio equivalent, the bulletin dip. Between them, 15 seconds is a good average. That can be all that ends up on air from a 15 minute interview which took 20 minutes to arrange, 30 minutes to set up and three hours to prepare. So is it worth it? Emphatically *yes*. The sound bite is the building block of the news report. It might be short, but it is *you* speaking and not the reporter. That means the message is undiluted and entirely yours. And if you have planned it well, the sound bite will convey your main point without any distracting flannel, in prime airtime, and with the added authority, cachet and credibility that comes from appearing on a news programme.

Media Campaigner for Act-Up, The AIDS Lobby in the USA: We have a woman... who was a television anchor at CBS news and... she gave all of the people who would go on television sound bite instructions, on how to speak to the media in the ten words of less they always like, to get everything in in a short amount of time.

Sound bite to Camera: The price of AZT is simply too high and because of that a lot of people don't have access to the drug and they're dying as a result; they're profiteering off our lives.[9]

If all they are looking for is a brief comment for a news bulletin, or you are one of several interviewees speaking in a news report, then the chances are that a sound bite will be all they want from you.

If you have followed the guidelines so far, you will have asked them how long the clip is expected to run and will have prepared your main message to length. Your performance in giving the soundbite will depend upon your preparation. If you know that's all they want, then you can write a good one and rehearse it well, aiming to put it across with both impact and conviction.

The purpose of the sound bite is *not* usually to give the facts of the news story. The introduction to the item should do that. The sound bite usually offers a comment, explanation or reaction. What the media wants is a strong, dramatic, reaction which will carry impact – but beware of ranting! The chosen sound bite is likely to be a statement of facts only in a developing news story, where what you say establishes some new point of information which takes the story further:

> The meeting has just finished and I can tell you our negotiations have been a success. We open as normal on Monday.

Many interviews follow the familiar pattern we discussed earlier:

- How do you see the benefits (of what is proposed)?
- How do you answer the problems and criticisms?
- What will your next action be?

Editors will be looking for sound bites to encapsulate those segments.

Relevance to the audience is everything. So if you are proposing a new development, the local media will want to know what's in it for their viewers. Next they will pick up on any controversy and ask you to justify the expense, the disruption, or the trouble it will cause. For their final clip they will often take the 'what's next?' angle, and ask you to look ahead to the coming stage in the unfolding story. This is your chance to keep the story on the boil.

If a major development in the saga is happening next week, such as meeting with union leaders to discuss layoffs, or a gathering of town planners to pass verdict on your plans for an abattoir in the ornamental rock gardens, then a sharp reporter will also ask you to record a piece to be used on the day in question in the bulletins running up to the meeting. And if they don't you ought to suggest it.

This is good extra publicity and saves you being bothered again at the time. What you will be asked to do is simply record a comment expressing your hopes for the meeting as though it was taking place that day. But be certain to let the media know if there are any changes to the plan and the meeting is dropped or shifted, otherwise it could all be very embarrassing...

The safer alternative is to arrange to call in nearer the time to give a preview piece and again after the meeting with your reaction. For the preview, arrange to call the evening before, which will give you access to the following day's morning audience – and if you're being interviewed for radio, that's the station's biggest.

There's no guarantee their first choice for the sound bite will coincide with yours, but if you've understood clearly the angle the news reporter is taking and exactly what he's looking for – *and* you managed to deliver that on tape – the chances are high that this is the sound bite he'll use.

The Labour Party Conference:
    Scripts of the Kinnock speech arrive five minutes after the Labour leader has started, and editor Rosaleen Hughes begins to mark obvious sound bites for a four-minute section that will open the evening's *Conference Day*. She says the clips are easy to choose: 'It's not too wordy, and that's unusual for Kinnock.'[10]

Many of the examples of quotes or comments used in these chapters would represent good, pithy sound bites. Be careful that you don't produce so many that they're spoiled for choice. Be mindful also that you won't be able to read from a statement. What you say will need careful preparation, but it will have to *sound* spontaneous.

Concentrate on polishing up your main message until it becomes a gleaming gem:

This order means more jobs, more wealth, more prosperity for the whole of this area... it's good news for Metrobus and it's a tremendous boost for the North East.

Masterclass

Alison Sergeant, News Editor, BBC Radio Cambridgeshire

If they are well prepared and know their subject they will find it a much less frightening experience than they think they will, because people in the media are usually *terribly* nice, they know it can be a nerve-wracking experience; they know the adrenalin is working 19 to the dozen, and they will do everything they can to make you feel comfortable and at ease before they wheel you in the studio and do the business with you.

Funnily enough, once you start speaking on air, adrenalin is a very good friend. It sharpens the mind wonderfully, and it helps you to say the things you really did mean to say. It's easy to say don't panic, but if you do get in a terrible muddle, providing it is not a matter of life and death, there's nothing wrong with making light of it. Just pause for a second and say, 'Hold on, let me put it another way' and start again.

Don't use copious notes. If you really are convinced you are going to forget your three key messages, write yourself three key words on the back of your hand, but don't bring in notes and read from them, and expect to sound natural, because you will fail.

Andrew Clayton, Editor, Business Daily, *Channel 4*

We're looking for straightforward answers to the questions we put, which are as honest as possible under the circumstances. If there are problems, we want people to address themselves to them.

We do two sorts of item. Either a straight interview which lasts about two minutes, or an interview which is going to be put in a package. In other words, the reporter will lead the subject on from the various bits of the interview that we use.

142

For the first sort we'll use three or four answers; for the second we're looking for thoughts which are 20 to 25 seconds long.

WOULD YOU TELL AN INTERVIEWEE THE LENGTH OF MATERIAL YOU WOULD BE EXPECTING?

Yes, we would. We'd tell him what was being done with it because then he knows *how* to do it. There's no point conducting an interview with somebody who's expecting to be able to talk on for ten minutes and finds it only lasts for two, because you don't cover the ground you're hoping to cover.

HOW WOULD YOU DESCRIBE THE IDEAL SOUND BITE?

What we want in 20 seconds is clarity, conciseness and a quick insight into why something is happening.

WHAT IF AN INTERVIEWEE DRIES UP?

Then it's the job of the interviewer to help him or her along; to come up with the phrase that will move them on to the next bit of the subject, and to make it sound as natural as possible. People very seldom dry up. If they do, it's as much the fault of the interviewer.

9

GETTING OUT OF A TIGHT CORNER

The occasion was the ambulance dispute, then in its seventeenth week. There was a short filmed report about the strike, then back in the studio [Jeremy] Paxman gave the latest stop-press headlines, after which he informed us, po-faced, that the Health Minister was with him in the studio. He swivelled his chair round to face his quarry, leaned forward purposefully and then remarked with unnerving affability: 'Well, you seem to have made rather a mess of this dispute, haven't you?'

Poor Mr Clarke. You could see he was thrown off balance, less by the words than by the unexpected tone: bantering, familiar and verging on insolence, but not for long. The longer the Minister's answers, the terser came the questions; and when the questions were parried, deflected or frankly avoided, back they came again. And again. Anglers who have witnessed a worm squirming at the end of a hook will appreciate how the rest of the interview was conducted.

Sue Arnold, *Radio Times*[1]

Most interviews are simply straightforward exchanges of information, but journalism can occasionally become a blood sport to be fought out in the most public of coliseums. You can either go meekly to the lions, or you can stand and fight. If you know *how* to stand your ground effectively, the marauding cats may hiss and spit, but they will eventually be forced to stalk off leaving the spectators cheering for you.

If you are to stand firm, you will need to prepare your ground beforehand. You'll need some mechanism in place to deal with a crisis: a chain of communication and an action plan that will produce one trained, qualified and well-prepared spokesman who will boldly step forward to face it out with the media.

Tricksters of the Trade

The BBC offers the following 'job description' of its interviewers:

Interviewers should not be 'aggressive, hectoring or rude [but] should appear tough-minded, sharp, sceptical, well-informed, but not partial, committed or emotionally attached to one side of the argument'.[2]

Quite so. But behind the professional mask of manners lurk primal instincts that can best be described as feral. The thrill of the chase seems to bring out a predatory streak in even the most mild-mannered of reporters.

A variety of techniques have evolved for closing in on the prey and preparing for the kill. Few will espouse the artless lunge for the jugular. And only those deserted by guile will sustain the ferocious frontal attack in the hope of breaking you down. Those with greater animal cunning will bide their time, stalking their prey, searching for some weakness – an undefended flank. The wilier still will beckon you with doe-eyed innocence until they've drawn you close enough to deliver the death blow. Or they'll bait the trap with some tempting lure and grinningly entice you towards it. Those higher up the evolutionary ladder will hand you the sword and invite you to fall on it yourself.

The Adversary

Why should the public on this issue believe *you*, a transient, here today, and, if I may say so, gone tomorrow politician...?
Sir Robin Day interviewing former British Defence Secretary John Nott during the Falklands Crisis. At which point Nott removed his microphone and stormed out.

Governments are in the business of actually *doing* things while the Opposition are in the business of *thinking* things. The actions of Governments have consequences which make it necessary for them to be questioned and criticised.

Brian Redhead, presenter, *Today* programme, Radio 4[3]

Adversarial interviews are commonplace for politicians and pressure groups, but a rarity with most businessmen. The premise is that politicians are elected and therefore answerable to their electorate, whose self-styled representatives are the media. The assumption is that you are shooting a line and the aim is to play devil's advocate to test your every weakness.

It is an approach which reflects the confrontational system of politics. Pressure groups and individuals calling for change and attempting to foist a point of view upon others can expect similar treatment.

Any politician that gets caught out in an interview must be an absolute prat... politics is all knockabout stuff anyway.

Steve Ellis

Businessmen are usually spared the third degree – until they come up with proposals which could be perceived as a threat to sections of the community, either locally or nationally. Then you can expect a string of 'Yes, but...' questions and to be called upon to justify your proposals. And quite rightly too.

The broadcast journalist in Britain has an obligation to show due impartiality, unlike colleagues in print who will often have to peddle their proprietor's editorial line. This has produced markedly different strands of journalism. Yet as only a moron is truly without opinions, the mask of impartiality can sometimes slip. Local journalists are often biased in favour of their audiences and regard themselves as the people's advocates or champions.

The media has an independent streak coupled with a willingness, even a duty to challenge, which is often interpreted as anti-authoritarian and therefore a threat to those with power, wealth or influence who are called on to justify their use of it. If the walls won't come down with the first blow, the same question may be asked again and again in different ways – or even identically – to try to shame you into submission. There are various methods of getting your blood up to try to rattle your composure:

- They may *overstate* the opposing view to sting you into a spirited defence.
- They may *bait* you by distorting your own arguments.
- They may *provoke* you by making you sound foolish.

Stay cool. If you treat it as a game, then it is less likely to become a blood sport. If you are feeling overawed, picture your inquisitor as an urchin with a runny nose, or, better still, as a Spitting Image puppet.

Various tricks will be employed to expose your weaknesses. Getting at you in an adversarial interview can be an effective way of riling you into saying something you shouldn't or breaking you down, but it lacks a certain *subtlety*.

The Buddy

Reporters like this *understand*. They will suck their teeth as you pour out your troubles, shake their head in sympathy and offer to buy you another beer. Everything about their manner suggests you can *relax* with them, they're on your side... until an hour's time when they will be playing the empathy game with your rival, trying to lull him into a false sense of security in order to get him to spill his secrets.

It's the approach tried often in union and management conflicts, where both sides can be grateful for a listening ear. Some journalists cultivate a wonderful, warm, bedside manner, but like doctors, their private thoughts about you could be unprintable. A sympathetic interview should never be taken as a guarantee of a sympathetic write-up. Beware... *every* reporter is a double agent.

The Barrister

'So to sum, up what you are saying is...' Listen hard to what the journalist thinks you are saying and beware of offering any word or gesture that might be taken as an endorsement. The summary might be fair, or it could contain an over-simplification or distortion that could be harmful to your cause.

There might be nothing malicious about it – the journalist is always trying to tidy up and to *clarify*, to explain things in simple terms, to cut up baby's dinner into bite-sized chunks. But be careful that their summary doesn't end up in print as *your* quote, unless you're happy that they have represented your case more succinctly than you.

The Manipulator

A reporter who has made up his/her mind in advance that the story is bad news is hardly going to tell you that. Anticipate the criticisms, try to read the clues in their questioning, and be sure to emphasise the *positive* aspects by promoting your message. Watch out as well that the summary they give doesn't try to shake you off the scent by slipping in some incorrect information amongst the bulk of the correct data:

> **Interviewer:** So what you're saying is that despite the effect on the environment and the increased traffic, the new factory will mean more jobs for local people, and you expect to have it finished when – in three months' time?

> **Developer:** No, it'll take a year.

> **Tomorrow's Paper:** Mr Fulcher believed the destruction to local woodland was justified. In his view, the extra jobs the factory would create would make up for the environmental damage to the area and the increased traffic congestion.

> Once the bulldozers move in, disruption resulting from building work is expected to last for a whole year.

148

The silly question about the completion date was designed to get your attention away from what had been said beforehand, so your failure to challenge the negative assertions about the environment and traffic could then be read as a passive endorsement.

That could have been avoided by anticipating the outcome and emphasising the positive:

> **Developer:** Let's take those points one at a time. The new factory will create more than a hundred new jobs, and this in an area where unemployment is running at 14 per cent. And local shopkeepers will find that more people with cash to spend will be a welcome boost to them too.
>
> Thanks to our tree planting programme, the loss to the environment will be short-lived, and careful landscaping will give the grounds a green and pleasant aspect.
>
> The work will be carried out as quickly as possible to cause the minimum disruption and should be completely finished within a year.

The Wise Monkey

The wise monkey will see, hear and ask selectively. This story is double-spaced in the reporter's mind and they won't thank you for complicating it with the facts. All they want from you is a quote to make their point. They've drafted it already, Now you just have to *say* it. Besides – they don't want to know any more than they need to for today's edition. Some good angles have to be saved for tomorrow's follow-up.

Notice the way journalists refer to news items as *stories*. The tendency is to reduce real life to the level of the comic-book, with heroes and villains, satisfying endings and only the simplest of sub-plots. Lack of space, shortage of airtime, and the overriding desire to *entertain* have much to answer for. You may want to play them at their own game by handing over your information in instalments to extend your coverage over several days. But jf you don't want to play, you don't have to. If you have information to give, don't wait for the monkey to *ask*. Remove his hands from his ears and *tell* him.

The Smiling Piranha

Never let the facts get in the way of a good story.

Anon.

The truth can sometimes spoil a neat hypothesis. Watch out for the set-up. The reporter has picked up a damn good story about you, and he/she is determined not to let anything knock it down, least of all *you*. They have to get your comment, but don't want to alert you to the seriousness of what's being said. So they'll gloss over the details as lightly as they can, their casual approach intended to lull you into a misplaced sense of security.

Typical of this is the one-sided complaint story, where the explanation, if there is one, can wait till tomorrow's edition. Fred Hammer bought his second-hand Ford from your garage two months ago. In the first week the headlights fizzled out, *something* was going thump-thump-thump round corners, and the engine was belching blue smoke. It went back to your garage three times before he was grudgingly satisfied with the repairs. The following day the big ends went and a wheel fell off and now you're callously refusing to give him a refund.

Clark Kent from the *Daily Blast* calls you up. His tone is cheerily apologetic: 'Sorry to bother you. Just wanted to check with you – we've had a Fred Hammer on to us about some car he bought from you. Says it's been back to you, but you're unwilling to fix it. Sounds like a bit of a misunderstanding. I'm sure there must be a perfectly good reason...'

And you briefly explain that the warranty has been invalidated so there is nothing you can do. Mr Kent seems well satisfied and you think nothing more of it.

On the next day's motoring page Fred Hammer appears in wide-angle looking glum besides his three-wheeled deathtrap. He has a neat if neanderthal line in invective which is quoted extensively, and each complaint is picked out and highlighted in a comprehensive list that runs on for several column inches. The piece ends with: 'A spokesman for Froxwood Motors said that as the warranty did not cover those problems, there was nothing they could do.'

Perhaps you *should* have pointed out that the warranty didn't cover your customer for stock-car racing...

150

If a journalist calls you about *anything* that could be detrimental to your organisation or your cause, always make sure you know the full details of the complaint or understand the other side of the issue before making your response. When you are satisfied you know the facts, take enough time to consider your reply. Never treat the issue lightly, even if the journalist in question *appears* to... To avoid being caught on the hop, anticipate controversy and be ready with your response.

The Rumour-monger

News is a barometer of change. No change is no news. So news thrives on extremes. Where the story involves an issue or dispute, the reporter will focus on the poles of the argument to highlight the contrast between the two sides. And there is usually only time for the highlights, which means that shades of nuance and subtlety of argument will be edited out.

By swinging between opposing viewpoints, stories can be kept seesawing for some time, as each reaction provides the opportunity to update a running-story where the facts themselves might be unchanged. Reaction stories are the cheapest form of news, and create a climate in which politicians – and speculation – thrive.

> We *understand* that many of your union members are In favour of the company's new offer and that pressure is mounting to end the industrial action...

> *Some people* are wondering how long the company can survive without firm orders. Three months has been *suggested*...

> There's been *speculation* that unless there's a show of support for you by the weekend, you're going to stand down...

The greatest source of speculation is the media itself, which is not beyond resorting to rumour-mongering to inject a head of steam into a static story. Confirmation may be rare, but even a denial is a fact of sorts and offers some new angle to run:

151

Union officials today *denied* that support was waning among their members and pledged to continue the long-running strike.

Redundancies now seem inevitable in the struggling ballbearing factory unless fresh orders can be found, the management *confirmed* today.

Patrick Penbury today *denied* suggestions that he was planning to resign by the weekend, unless there was a concrete show of support for his position.

First ask where the rumour and speculation has come from. *Who* says; *who* suggests, *who* speculates... 'A good journalist never reveals his sources' is a reporter's way of saying no comment, but if there is some substance to the rumour and the source is not in confidence, they might just tell you. Either way, consider your reply with care. Each of the three questions above was designed to annoy its subject and provoke an immoderate reaction.

If the rumour is on target (even if the source is really only the reporter) then don't allow your hand to be forced ahead of time. A denial now will be used against you later. No-comment will sound as though you have something to hide and will serve to confirm the rumour. Better to be non-committal and suggest a responsible reason for prevaricating:

We are still considering our course of action. It would be unwise to say anything at the moment that might pre-empt or jeopardise the outcome.

If the rumour is off-target, then avoid giving a negative reply but use the opportunity to put over a point that is both positive and active:

Our members are determined to succeed because our cause is just and we will hold out until the management accept that.

Our sales force is going flat out for new orders, and it has never been as vital for everyone in the company to pull together at a time that is difficult for many firms.

There is a lot to be done here, and I have every intention of continuing to serve as long as my services continue to be required.

Contrast that with a response that is in the negative:

The strike is not crumbling.

I have no intention of resigning by the weekend.

If the rumour is false, avoid repeating it, because speculation gains shape and substance when it is put into your words, even if only in the form of a denial. The audience will simply assume there is no smoke without fire.

How to Handle Your Interviewer

Before taking things further, let's summarise the ground we've covered so far in this chapter:

- The journalist will play devil's advocate, and use a variety of tricks to try to expose the weaknesses in your argument.
- Anticipate controversy.
- Understand the opposing argument.
- Have your response to each point ready.
- Always emphasise the positive elements of your message.
- If they don't ask for your information, tell them anyway.
- Deal with speculation by making a *positive* denial or clear confirmation.
- Never *react* to the media, only *respond*.

In her useful book, *How to Take On The Media*,[4] Sarah Dickinson identifies what she describes as the key components you should put over in the crisis interview irrespective of the questions they ask you:

Do:
- show concern and sympathy for anyone affected;
- offer assurance that the matter will be thoroughly investigated;

- reaffirm your organisation's excellent safety/hygiene/employment record; and
- assert that your standards are well above the statutory minimum.

Don't:
- Speculate on the cause of the problem;
- Admit blame or negligence; or
- Commit your company to compensation.

The rest of this section assumes that you're being interviewed on TV or radio where not only *what* you say, but the *way* you say it comes under public scrutiny. Otherwise, the suggestions apply equally to newspaper interviews. There are two golden rules: don't tell whoppers – and never lose your temper.

On Being Economical with the Truth

We are now in the grip of an almost Goebbels-like industry – the industry of professional lying has taken over our lives.
Film maker Marcel Ophuls

However carefully you have planned; however sound the rapport you thought you had established with your interviewer, however routine the exchange *ought* to be... sometimes things can go off course, and you will need to steer the interview away from troubled waters without resorting to out-and-out deception and downright manipulation...

There are times when... there is a strong temptation to deny everything. The short answer is, don't – and don't allow your management to do so either. If you or any of the representatives of your organisations do lie, your reputation in the media will be shattered and its loss will precede you into whatever industry you go. It is very rare for the truth not to emerge, given time, and once a journalist has been castigated by his editor for believing your lies he will, understandably, never trust you again. He will be suspicious of everything you

154

and your organisation have to say and will tell his associates to be wary too.

Judith Ridgeway, *Successful Media Relations*[5]

Tell the truth. People aren't fools you know. The viewing public will make up their own minds and it is an increasingly sophisticated public and they are increasingly adept at spotting evasions and lies, so I think you embark on that course at your own peril really.

Jeremy Paxman

Never Lose Your Temper

When an interview becomes a scene, I always think 'Yippee great copy!'

Lynn Barber

Stay cool and collected, even if you can't be calm.

David Morgan Rees[6]

If your temper goes out of the window, your credibility will vanish with it. Don't let your hackles rise. The BBC warns its journalists that if there is any emoting to be done, it must come from you and not from them. That's how *they* play it. Lose your temper and you've lost the game. However, it can be in your interest to run a little warm, providing you keep well under boiling point. Many a good journalist keeps a sharpened goad in her handbag. Lynn Barber again:

> Towards the end of an interview I try to vary the emotional temperature a bit – perhaps to provoke the subject to anger if we have been unduly cosy hitherto... Asking [the question] in a 'hostile' form will often elicit a more passionate and actually more sympathetic answer than asking it in its bland form. Interviewees are often much better served by hostile questions than by friendly ones: forced to defend themselves hard, they are far more likely to appeal to the reader. The really deadly questions are the dulcet ones.[7]

Short of blowing a fuse, the other extreme to be avoided on radio or TV is cosying up to your interviewer too much. First name terms can sound chummy or conspiratorial, but can be a handy minor put-down, as the use of the first name implies a degree of knowing: 'Now Jeremy, I'm *sure* you know better than that...'

Conversely, formal titles or surnames; 'As I was saying, Sir Robin...' or 'Quite so, Mr Dimbleby,' sound out of place and pompous. Just answer the questions and don't refer to the interviewer as anything. Be pleasant and responsive to your interviewer, but remember, it's not really them you're talking to – it's the viewer.

Always assume that audience sympathy lies with the interviewer – at least to begin with; after all, he or she has probably been a welcome guest in the home for years, and in media terms, familiarity breeds content. If you are arrogant or abrasive towards the presenter they've come to regard as one of the family, the audience will instinctively regard that hostility as aimed at *them*.

Public sympathy will always swing against the aggressor, whoever it happens to be. Which doesn't mean you should allow yourself to be walked over! Instead, if your interviewer gets hot, you should stay cool (never cold!); if he/she becomes aggressive you should emerge as the voice of reason; if he/she is negative, you should be positive. If he/she treats you with disrespect, respond like a long suffering but kindly uncle or aunt to a younger nephew who's got a bit above his station. Never enter into a head-on clash with your interviewer. No sensible general sends his troops to fight in enemy territory, under the enemy's conditions and on the enemy's terms. It's the interviewer's job to pit your argument against opposing points of view. Never take it personally or allow yourself to feel got at.

Persistence is often called for, harassment is not.

BBC Guidelines

The interviewer's professional impartiality means if you make a point strongly or represent a vested interest, he or she is virtually *obliged* to put the opposite point with almost as much vigour. Treat it as a sophisticated game of words played by professionals. If it does threaten to become a sparring match, keep it a good-humoured one.

Don't get uptight or petulant if you want to win and retain audience sympathy.

One ex-BBC-TV producer who now runs a school for teaching politicians how to appear on television has a rule that you can be rude to an interviewer only if he has been rude to you at least three times!

Denis MacShane, *Using the Media*[8]

Loss of temper is loss of control. And that in itself can become the story: 'Revealed, the amazing BBC recording of Labour leader's outburst of swearing' was the headline that greeted allegations that Neil Kinnock had expleted one 'God', one 'Christ', two 'bloody's and a 'cocked it up' in a recording for Radio 4's *The World at One*. Who remembers that the 'it' in question was the economy... ?

Killer Questions

Mr Heath, how *low* does your personal rating from your own supporters have to go before you consider yourself a liability to the party you lead?

Robin Day

A warm grin and a firm handshake when you meet your interviewer is no indication that what is to follow will resemble a cosy chat. Remember the grinning piranha. First questions can often be the toughest, and these will set the scene for the entire interview:

So you're putting the rail fares up again – by double the rate of inflation – and you think you can get away with it because there's no competition – is that it?

Of course, you're prepared for trouble, so you're not taken aback, but your answer is vital. You have to counter the argument, reassure the audience and promote your viewpoint. In other words, you have to tilt the balance back in your favour – and do it in your first answer, or the rest of the interview will be a rout:

157

Nobody likes to put up their prices – least of all us. Because we are in competition – people vote with their feet, and Britannia Rail values its customers. In the past year we've introduced many brand new engines and brand new carriages. Standards of comfort and safety are higher then ever before. But it's cost us. Oh, we could revamp the old trains, but we still need new ones to be able to offer more services, and our customers deserve the best. Hence the rise. And we know full well that the only way to *keep* our customers is to keep improving our service.

Keep the negative in its place by presenting the positive first – right at the beginning of the interview and irrespective of what they ask you:

Interviewer: Can you confirm that you're considering 500 redundancies?

Interviewee: We have a workforce of more than 5,000 and a plant that has recently been expanded. All the signs were that demand would grow and more orders would come in – and I believe they will. But the unexpectedly high interest rates that have taken the city by surprise and which have hit consumers and house owners so badly have hit us too. People no longer have the cash in their pockets and demand is down. Ordinary people have had to cutback and so must we. If we didn't we'd overstretch and put the rest of our workforce at risk – and we have absolutely no intention of doing that. So, yes, I'm afraid that this situation has meant 500 jobs will have to go. It's deeply regrettable, but we have no choice, and I can assure the staff we have to lose that our redundancy terms will be most generous.

Watch out for killer questions. When a reporter is about to go in for the kill, they'll sometimes try to get you to establish a fact which they can use against you:

Interviewer: You say you're taking steps to deal with pollution from your factory. Let's be clear. *How much* pollution? Exactly how much green sludge is your factory pumping out into the river?

Interviewee: Well, any amount would be too much. As I've already said, we're well within EC guidelines, but what we want to move towards is a business that, as practically as possible, is non-polluting and which is putting something positive *back* into the environment. And that's what we've begun to achieve with landscaping and intend to take further with our clear waters policy.

Again, counter negative suggestions with positive assertions and get straight to the point. The art of turning difficult questions to your advantage is summed up beautifully by Bland and Mondesir in their book, *Promoting Yourself On Television And Radio.*[9]

1.   Think of something you'd like to say if you were given 15 seconds of free television time.
2.   Think up the nastiest, most loaded, antipathetic question about the subject.
3.   Put the two together!

Correcting the Interviewer

People are being prevented from saying what they really want to say by being constantly interrupted and deflected by opposition and awkward questions. I am against the theatre of embarrassment.

Jeremy Isaacs, Chief Executive, Channel 4[10]

Faulty facts

Your interviewer may be well-intentioned, and may even consider herself well-briefed, but sometimes, inevitably, she will get her facts wrong. If the error is important enough, pick up on it straight away. If you wait until you've answered the question it may be too late to swing things round: the interviewer may be pressing ahead with

159

another point, or you may be so taken up answering the question that you forget to register your objection. By then the argument will have moved on, the point will have been made, and the wrong impression will have been fixed in the audience's mind.

Don't dive in to correct every little mistake; it'll make you appear petty and pedantic. Only correct major mistakes that are critical to your argument, and then make your correction in a good-natured way. An interviewer will sometimes move things forward by stating facts that lay the foundation for the next question:

> Now, losing this export order means your factory won't be working at full capacity, and the union is afraid that could lead to layoffs. How many jobs are at risk?

Don't interrupt the interviewer, but pick up on the point as soon as the question has been put:

> No, I'm afraid that's incorrect. The Hanningtons' plant will continue to work at *full capacity*. What the loss of this order means is that we won't be able to proceed with our *expansion* plans for the plant. *All* jobs on existing orders will be preserved – there's no question about that – though contractors who've been working on this particular export order will not – unfortunately – have their contracts renewed.

Only go as far as interrupting the interviewer when they *consistently* and *persistently* get facts wrong. That's the time that any reasonable person would begin to lose patience. Audience sympathy will be with you and cutting in will help you regain control of the interview while demonstrating that you're not a doormat.

If the interviewer should try to interrupt you, don't pause to let them in, as conventional good manners may require, but rebuff them gently by adopting a determined tone, raising your voice slightly, fixing their eye with yours and carrying on until you've reached the end of your sentence or finished making your point. The onus is on them to produce an intelligible interview, and they won't get that by talking over what you have to say.

9. Getting Out of a Tight Corner

Flawed opinions

Interviewers often test an argument or claim by putting forward contradictory opinions. To maintain impartiality the broadcaster may distance himself from an opinion by attributing it to another authority:

> Dr Kenneth Jackman has gone on the record as saying your scheme is doomed to failure. He's called it 'ill-advised, under-funded and unimaginative'. What do you say to that?

Of course, as you keep yourself fully informed about what your opponents are saying, remarks like Dr Jackman's will come as no surprise. You'll be expecting that viewpoint to be represented in an interview – if it isn't, your interviewer isn't doing his job. Again, you need to *anticipate* opposition by preparing for it.

Sometimes the interviewer will put forward opinions that are not attributed. The standard form for this is a question beginning with:

> Some people will say that..., or, Opponents might argue...

Again, be prepared for this and have your answer ready. And if you're certain exactly who has been expressing that contradictory opinion, then gain a control point by revealing your knowledge and exposing your opponent:

> Yes, Or Kenneth Jackman of Cyberco has made that point several times, but then he would, wouldn't he – after all, Cyberco is a direct competitor.

Show that you've faced up to the opposing points of view, you understand them, and that you've found good and reliable grounds for thinking differently. Assuming your point of view is sound, considered and positive, you should project it as such. Your opponent's objections will appear ill-thought out; precipitate and negative. It is better tactics to project your position positively than to attack an opponent's. But if the position you are representing is shaky, then why have you set yourself up to push that point of view on a TV programme? If there are weaknesses, a good interviewer will expose them, however much flack or flannel you put up.

161

That means there's no room for complacency about what your organisation is doing or what your opponents are saying. But unless you believe in your position you'll never succeed in persuading others to believe in it too. Worse still, in the long term they'll cease to believe in you.

Dealing with the Opposition

If you know that your interview is to appear in a recorded report with comments from others putting opposing or contrasting points of view, ask for a transcript of what the other interviewees say in the report. If the producer obliges it's to your advantage, because you can tailor your comments in response to what has been said and counter their arguments. Your request might be turned down if the other interviews have yet to take place, or if the producer protests that this would give you an unfair advantage over the others who've had to make their comments without the benefit of hearing what *you* had to say. But it's worth asking, and increasingly, government ministers are insisting on it before agreeing to give the interview:

> If a minister will appear in segments, the demand is for each piece of interview preceding his or her contribution to be read to him or her in advance. A smooth practitioner then inserts references to what has gone before, thus giving an impression of being in charge of the programme.
>
> BBC World Service Managing Director, John Tusa[11]

The media is becoming justifiably wary of this form of manipulation, and few pressure groups or company spokesmen carry the clout of a government minister! But even if the producer does draw the line at revealing other comments in the report; providing you understand what the interview is about and know who else they're planning to talk to, you should have a good idea of their arguments and be able to emphasise the positive aspects of your own case and put over your message:

Interviewer: Professor Westheimer has called your plans to provide low-cost housing units in community *pyramids*

162

absurd, ridiculous and technically impossible. What do you say to that?

Interviewee: I'm sure people like the learned Professor would have sneered at the original pyramids in Egypt, and *they're* still standing! Today we have the benefit of modern technology. Our designs are superb, our plans are cost-effective – *and they're attractive.* People are telling us they want to live there – and how often do you hear that said about a tower block?

Available from all leading estate agents! The answer uses an ironic analogy for good humoured impact, and instead of defending the argument point by point, the interviewee goes on the offensive to put across his main message.

What if they don't ask the Right Questions?

Working for a company like Shell you *can't* know all the answers, and you have to be honest and say, 'I'm very sorry, but I don't know the answer to that.' If they are being arrogant we don't fly off the handle with them, we are patient and we just have to reiterate the points that we are making. We have to use the skill that politicians use, although not too much...

John Pike

If, after all the pre-chat and the trouble you took to clarify the area of questions before agreeing to the interview, you're still caught out, then either you need more training, or someone's been pulling the wool over your eyes. While there's still time and the interview is continuing, you'll need to turn it around to somehow get your message across. Obviously it's no good ignoring the question, because the question will only be asked again. You'll need to touch on the question briefly and then go on immediately in the same sentence to make your own point before your interviewer can cut in:

Interviewer: But other share flotations have been less successful. Take Westbury Widgets, for example, the public just weren't buying...

Interviewee: You've got to get your marketing right along with your product, and we believe we have – the product is good, the prospects are good and we can market it in confidence as a sound investment offering a potentially high return for a modest layout.

If a question is clearly spurious and irrelevant to the subject you've agreed to discuss, then politely but firmly say so:

That's not what we're discussing here. What you've asked me to talk about is...

That's not relevant. The important issue here is...

It's a technique used by seasoned campaigner Des Wilson:

I always go on very clear in my mind of the main points I want to make, and make them almost irrespective of what the question is. Or the question can simply be turned around, even abruptly, by simply saying, 'Well, to be frank with you, I don't think that's the real question. The real question is...' So you can take over the questioning role yourself, lay down the question, and then answer it.

Sometimes an interviewer who is lazy, inexperienced, or who hasn't had much time to prepare can be quite happy for you to do that, because you're partly helping them do their job.

However...

I'm sick to death of hearing on the *Today* programme some silly politician crudely saying, 'Before I answer that, Mr Redhead, I must first tell you...' If I hear that damn line again, I'm going to scream.

Steve Ellis

Politicians who have, by and large, mastered the art of ignoring political cross examination, turning their appearances into monologues of self-justification and polemic have succeeded in so reducing the appeal of politics on television that the dreaded phrase, 'Before I answer your question may I just say...' drives the viewer to switch channels.

UK Press Gazette[12]

If prevarication is to be employed, do so with subtlety.

Squaring up to Trouble

The failure to answer or even address the questions asked is not a wise move for people who want to win the hearts and minds of a mass audience. Viewers and listeners know perfectly well when an interviewee is evading a question. They are free to draw their own conclusions about the motives, honesty and integrity of the person concerned.

Max Atkinson, *The Independent*[13]

Sometimes you'll be asked questions which you can't answer or to which it would be detrimental to attempt to reply. When the interview is being arranged, if you detect a real threat that the interview could be damaging, *and* you suspect more harm would be done by giving the interview than refusing it – turn it down.

Assuming you're going ahead, then it's usually possible to deflect difficult questions, but there's a danger your audience will spot your tactic and wonder what you're trying to hide. It's the difference between tax avoidance and tax evasion. Avoidance is acceptable and no-one knows about it, but evasion is an offence. Both get you off the hook for the time being, but if they suspect the evasion, they'll get you in the end.

What you must do is recognise your danger zones. Anticipate difficult questions and prepare an answer for them. Plan a safe answer that will deflect the questions as openly and as honestly as possible, similar to the way we discussed for avoiding an outright denial. Take time to come up with a suitable form of words:

> As you know, talks are taking place at the moment, and the last thing I want to do is to say anything that would prejudice those important discussions.
>
> These are early days. We're well aware of the important issues involved and we're exploring them carefully. When our research has been completed our findings will be made known. It wouldn't be helpful- or proper – to speculate beyond that at the moment.
>
> It would be quite irresponsible for me to comment about that right now...

Don't be a stonewall. Be human, be open. If your reluctance to speak is clearly a responsible gesture, then it would seem *ir*responsible for the interviewer to press the point. If you're taking trouble to be as open as you can, then your interrogator is unlikely to take to you like a crowbar to a clam shell. To do so would be to turn the audience against him, believes Bud Evans of *Today*:

> If the interviewer continued to press the question and the interviewee maintained the same stance, there would come a point at which the audience would be more restless with the interviewer than the interviewee. If the interviewee gave in an honest way the reason why an answer can't be given, the interviewer would be a fool to carry on for too long.
>
> We can ask it twice. We can ask it three times. But we can't ask it four times because people would be bored and write to us about what a rude and persistent interviewer that was!

A view supported by Max Atkinson in *The Independent* newspaper:

> The more the interviewer persists... the greater the risk of being seen as aggressive, hostile, obsessive, narrow-minded or impolite.[14]

Sometimes a tricky interviewer will insist on asking you questions you've already said you won't discuss. He/she knows you won't be drawn about them, and they have decided to play a different game.

What they are trying to do is to *expose* your no-go areas to the audience.

Don't fall into the trap of saying, 'But we agreed not to talk about that!' as your audience will have a right to wonder why and will always imagine the worst.

> The tendency has been for party managers to try increasingly for assurances about subjects to be covered or excluded. Gerald Kaufman, Shadow Foreign Secretary, threatened to walk out of BBC's *Breakfast Time* if Jeremy Paxman raised a report in *The Sun* that the Kinnocks were paid up members of CND. He failed to get such an assurance, gave a rambling answer when the question was put, and left the studio, warning Paxman that he'd be sorry.
>
> John Cunningham, *The Guardian*[15]

The better approach is to field the question and try to use it as a platform for making a positive statement. A similar approach is to sidestep the main issue by picking up on another opening given by the interviewer. This can sometimes shift the balance in your favour:

Interviewer: The resignation of three of your top managers in as many weeks must surely be a reflection on your company's policy and your own management style – they don't like it!

Interviewee: On the contrary; our managers are hand-picked for their expertise, their drive and their ambition. They're excellent at their work and we value their contribution enormously. But these same robust qualities mean that many will make their mark and move on – and good luck to them! We've trained them well and they've served us well. And this sort of movement encourages the next generation of leaders to make moves on up. I'm sure the same sort of thing happens in the BBC all the time, as it will wherever you have talented and ambitious people.

As far as company policy is concerned, our overriding aim remains the same – we strive for success and we refuse to settle for less than the very best.

The reference to the BBC in the middle was intended to be disarming. A light touch may not win an argument, but it will increase audience sympathy. It wins you a control point, and it also makes it more difficult for the interviewer to maintain their aggressive stance – the last thing they want is the audience to turn against them.

Another useful deflection is to acknowledge the point – where it would not be damaging to do so – and then move on:

Yes, I agree, but of far more importance is...

Fair point, but what we must also recognise is...

That's OK as far as it goes, but as you know, the issue is wider than that...

The martial arts may offer a clue. In judo, the art is to hold your ground and use your aggressor's own momentum against him by throwing him off balance. Try a turn of the tail:

Of course we want this strike to end as quickly as possible, but there's an even bigger issue at stake...

The problem is obvious – that's why we've launched a full inquiry to look into it and propose whatever changes might be necessary...

Well that's precisely why we're holding an inquiry, and until the inquiry makes its findings it would be unwise of me to discuss the details...

Ah, but you've got to look at this in context...

It's an interesting point and worth coming back to, but more important than that...

If you don't want to concede their point, then you could leave it dangling and refer to another issue or precondition that leads in to the point you want to make:

Ah, but there are other factors to be taken into consideration...

But the issue here is wider than that...

But there's another point we have to consider first...

If you want to be more assertive in your argument (remember, assertion – not aggression), you could deflect more strongly, with:

Let's not jump to conclusions. If we look at the background to this...

Now there's a danger here of putting two and two together and making 22! Let's just look at the facts...

Let's get this straight. This issue is not about policy, nor is it about personalities; it's about success. As a company develops, so does its personnel. And as that company moves on, often they do too. To better things. For businesses and individuals, there's nothing worse than standing still. What we all want is progress. That's what we've got, and it's *good*.

Notice that at no point does the interviewee directly challenge, contradict or accuse the interviewer. 'Let's look at the facts' is a world apart from saying, 'You've got your facts wrong' or, 'Why don't you deal with the facts...' or even, 'Call yourself a journalist? I thought reporters were supposed to deal with facts, not fiction...' – not recommended, even if you are in the right, as the audience will think you're picking on the interviewer and they will turn against you.

At no time should you just go in for slavishly repeating the same neat pre-packaged answer. Apart from sounding like a coin in the slot machine, your response will come over as knee-jerk and insincere. The spectacle of the former British Prime Minister, Margaret Thatcher, blinking hard during an extended interview about the resignation of her Chancellor, and repeating like an incantation the phrases: 'Ministers decide and advisors advise' and 'the Chancellor's position is unassailable' resulted in media accusations that Mrs Thatcher had well and truly ducked the issue. Her own resignation was already on the horizon.

Much of what we have said so far deals with averting head-on confrontation. But you need to do more than that – the interview has to be steered away from trouble and back to the message you want to put over.

Interviewer: Let's just talk about the long-term implications of this for your company... aren't you in danger of overreaching yourselves?

Interviewee: Every graduate of business school knows the dangers of expanding too quickly can be as great as just sitting on your laurels and doing nothing. And we've never been ones for that. A *carefully planned* expansion scheme is the way to maximise our growth at the minimum risk; to safeguard existing jobs and pave the way for new work to be brought into the community.

Don't go on the defensive

Avoid appearing defensive. If the audience pick it up – which they will- they'll be convinced that 'here is somebody with something to hide'. Don't allow yourself to be trapped like a rat in a corner fighting to defend your position. You've already made up your mind about what you need to put across to make this interview work for you – now simply make sure you say it.

One difficulty can be that if you've prepared properly you'll be well aware of any weaknesses in your position. These will be the areas you're trying to avoid. As a result, the focus of your attention could easily rest upon them. But your preparation will have anticipated questions that stray into the danger zone and you should have found ways of providing positive answers to them.

Remember: the weaknesses may loom large to you, but you're closer to the problem than almost anyone in the audience. And you're also closer to the aspects of your business, your argument and your position that are good and positive and can be promoted. Do so. Obviously you should avoid braggadocio, but no salesman ever clinched a deal with false modesty:

Interviewer: This development is being built on a nature reserve. Conservationists have called it a tragedy for the countryside. Couldn't you build it somewhere else?

Interviewee: The town planners and the public inquiry have agreed that this is the best possible place for a new hypermarket. And we think they've made an excellent decision. Access is superb. The store, car parking and new roads can be built without disrupting a soul. No-one's home will have to be bought up and not a single shop will be closed. There'll be superb new shopping facilities for the people of Filbury – much needed for many years – *and* 600 new jobs. And it'll be landscaped and buildings hidden from view by the hundreds of new trees that we're planting. So what was once wasteland will be woodland. And we've called in experts to help us find and save the wild plants and the animals who live there and carefully relocate them out of harm's way.

Notice the reference to higher authorities at the outset. It's just a subtle form of taking the credit while spreading the blame.

Media consultant Dina Ross advocates taking the pressure off yourself by claiming the support of others:

My company is often called in to advise corporations whose spokesmen fidget about uncomfortably when asked hot potato questions by the press. Our advice has always been to come up with a corporate message, sometimes allied to other leaders in their industry.[16]

Beware the pregnant pause

The pregnant pause is a great device which interviewers use to get someone to keep talking in the hope that they'll land themselves firmly in it. The reporter senses that she is penetrating your defences. The answer you've given to the question is a model one. You've fended her off with a brief but positive sounding statement – but it's just a bit too slick. You think you're in the clear. You pause to let her ask the next question – only she doesn't. She pauses too. One

171

eyebrow is raised and she transfixes you with a gimlet eye. Your smile freezes. She knows. The pause lingers... and then you blurt out what she wanted to hear:

Of course, not *everyone's* in favour of our proposal but...

or

Well, there has been *some* discussion about the effect on the environment, but...

or

Of course, *some* jobs will have to go...

The pause is an uncomfortable little blighter. It's put there to make you sweat; to see if you'll cough; to give you enough rope... But after a couple of seconds – if that – the pause becomes even more uncomfortable for the interviewer. There's nothing broadcasters loathe more than dead air. One of the first rules of broadcasting is if there is a silence – fill it. And if *you* don't, rest assured your interviewer will, and that the next question will follow as surely as night follows day.

Take care to avoid setting man-traps for yourself – don't volunteer information that might be used against you. Instead, use the pause as a chance to come across with one of your key points, by using a bridge such as:

- Just as important...
- What we mustn't forget...
- What we have to remember is...
- The other point is...

Beware the Death Blow

'One final word...' beware the final summary that deals the death blow. The end of the interview will leave the audience with their most lasting impression. The reporter is well aware of that, and may decide to come in for the kill in the dying moments when it's supposedly too late for you to do anything about it:

Interviewer: So, 300 breadmakers out on strike, your union is refusing to talk to the management and meanwhile we all go hungry. Mr Baker, thank you very much.

Don't stand for that! You've got a few seconds to put the picture right before the director cuts to the next piece. Get in *fast*. Hit back with a short positive statement that reinforces your message, not a negative one that reinforces *theirs*:

Not: Now, come on! I've just told you, the *management* won't talk to *us*. Furthermore, we gave them three clear warnings – one, that if they persisted in their intransigent attitude... (faded out by director)

But: Oh, we'll talk – just as soon as the *management* agrees to negotiate. Then perhaps we can all get back to the business of making bread.

Troubleshooting Recorded Interviews

Once recorded there is, in general, no unassailable right to withdraw permission for use of an interview.
BBC Guidelines for Factual Programmes[17]

You have one advantage if the interview is recorded. In a dire emergency you can pause it, interrupt it or stop it altogether luxuries not afforded to those going live. If the interview is about a crucial issue, have with you in the room a colleague who understands it and knows what's at stake. Then, if the interview takes a really bad turn, he or she can step in and discreetly interrupt – *as a last resort*. Part of the interview will have to be recorded again and the media will need your co-operation to do that. Be careful, though, they might call your bluff and multiply your embarrassment by screening the intervention, as happened to former British Prime Minister, Harold Wilson. More usefully, your colleague can remind you if you've left out anything of importance, and the two of you can bring gentle pressure to bear to shoot an extra question.

Never routinely ask to repeat an interview in the hope of producing a better performance. On most occasions your first take will be the best, because the flow of adrenalin will have made you sharper. Reporters know that, so they usually refuse retakes. Besides, they have a deadline to meet, and you should already have rehearsed the interview.

What worries interviewees most is if they say something wrong then it is there on tape preserved for all time. With newspaper interviews you can always deny them afterwards, but here, it's firm and it's on tape, and it's stark horror if you get the emphasis slightly wrong.

We've never had a problem. If they say something that is genuinely wrong, then we can, of course, retake the question. If we feel he merely wants to cover something up, then we'd say, 'Terribly sorry, you've said it and it's a matter of public record.' We'd be tough if we felt that somebody was trying to cover something up. We'd be understanding if it was merely something that was wrong.

Andrew Clayton

Don't forget to make your own recording.

'By the way, that's off-the-record...'

If you say beforehand, 'This is off-the-record, or background', then they are obliged to respect that. Sometimes people tell you things off-the-record and say, 'Well, off-the-record, the score is this, but I'm not going to talk about it in the interview, and if you ask me I'll deny it,' but it's not that common. I think if you are told information in confidence, then you are obliged to respect it.

Jeremy Paxman

Even if the reporter is the most congenial chap in the world, who sympathises deeply with your point of view and has wined you and dined you and fretted over you; never let your guard down for a moment. Don't allow yourself to be lulled into a false sense of security. Like policemen, journalists are never off duty. Even the cuddliest can turn out to be a carnivore with sharp incisors. Your words will be shouted from the roof tops. Think before you speak and never confide your innermost secrets to a news reporter, even if he/she does appear to be on your side.

If you are being entertained by a reporter, perhaps as the prelim to an interview, the same rules about alcohol apply as in the studio – don't. Treat every meeting with a news reporter as on-the-record. Never give off-the-record information wherever a mike is in sight. If you're at a location interview, make sure the recorder is switched off first if you really must bare your soul. If you are saying something in confidence which you don't want relayed to the world, then you will need to follow the rules of the game – and make sure beforehand that you are both playing by the same rulebook.

The Ground Rules

I've had some cases where people have told me stuff clearly on-the-record, and when it's in print they've obviously regretted it, or their boss comes down on them and says it's company policy not to talk to the press. Then they've denied it all and claimed fabrication. That's more common than you'd realise, but then that's not my fault – it's theirs.

Russell Hotten

Make sure that you state clearly that the discussion is off-the-record *before* you spill the beans, and that you both agree *exactly* what that means. It was the failure of a contact to do just that that delivered reporters Woodward and Bernstein their famous Watergate coup. It's no good whining to a reporter after you have finished baring your soul that, 'By the way, all that was just between the two of us.' News reporters are walking megaphones.

Off-the-record briefings can take a number of different forms. They can give background information which the journalist will have to check out and get on-the-record from another source before running the story, or they can be to give information for publication which can in no shape or form be traced back to you. This is known as a *non-attributable* briefing. The parliamentary lobby system in the UK works on that basis. It is a useful way of leaking proposals to sound out the reaction before claiming the credit for yourself.

If you are happy for the information to be used but don't want to be attributed as its source, then the reporter will give your words and attribute them vaguely, by saying something like: 'A high-ranking official said today...' or 'Sources close to the Chief Executive say...'.

Journalists will always want to attribute what they say, because they are paranoid that someone will accuse them of making it all up. But if this level of attribution is still too close for comfort you may want to keep the information *strictly* non-attributable with no hints that could identify either you or your position. The phrase the reporter would then use would be something like: 'It is understood that...' or, 'I have reason to believe that...' Agree the form or words. Your risk of exposure is than diminished, unless it is obvious to those in the know that you were the only one who could have passed on that information...

Be absolutely certain that both you and the reporter come to a mutual understanding of what is meant by off-the-record. The rules of the game differ because there *are* no rules and no-one around to enforce them. You're on dangerous ground. The onus is on you to clarify, because the press will naturally want to push a story as far as they can. Try to avoid mixing on-the-record with off-the-record. That is a recipe for confusion. Your safest bet is to either go totally on or totally off. Preferably the former.

Investigative TV reporters will sometimes want to push things even further. To add high drama to an exposure story they may ask you to reveal all in anonymous interview, shot in silhouette against a bright window, with your face blocked out by an electronic mosaic, or even with your voice electronically scrambled to sound like Daffy Duck.

You'd have to be daffy or desperate to even consider it. *Bow out gracefully*. Leave that kind of tacky treatment to supergrasses and revolutionaries. Besides, it can be remarkably easy to see through those disguises by turning up the brightness of the picture or squinting to make out the face beneath the mosaic.

Doorstepping

Techniques such as 'chasing with the camera'... and car door interviews, should be justified by a clear public interest and used only when important material could not have been obtained in any other way.

BBC Guidelines for Factual Programmes

There is a kind of interview which you may not want to give, but which the media is determined to take. So determined that they'll wait all day outside your home, office or negotiating hall for you to step outside, before besieging you for a comment. These are the interviews where what people really want to say is 'push off' – or words to that effect – but where they usually end up saying 'No comment'. Say neither.

The best approach is to pause just long enough to give a brief but beautifully rehearsed non-committal comment – there is a distinction – and then move on. Stay polite and don't get panicked. As we said earlier, denials and negative statements are out. 'No comment' sounds tight-lipped and evasive. If circumstances mean you can't talk now, be human, these people have been waiting in the cold and the wet for hours – most journalists hate doorstepping almost as much as you do. Tell them why you can't talk:

I'm sorry, the court won't allow us to talk about that at the moment, the case is *sub judice.*

Try out the warm but apologetic smile perfected by Ronald Reagan and say something like:

Obviously it wouldn't be helpful to discuss it right now. The discussions are taking place in *there*, and as soon as we can report any progress, I'm sure you folks will be the first to know.

We're still talking, and that's what counts.

Agreed, the words say nothing at all. The important thing is that you explain *why* you can't explain.

There will always be a natural conflict between journalism and public relations. Dan Rather of CBS TV said in dealing with the media, there's one of three things I can say:

- I know, and I can tell you
- I know, but I can't tell you, or
- I don't know.

The second is always the hardest; then you've got to tell them *why*.

It's a person's right not to answer questions, but I have a right as a journalist to ask them. Sometimes they will rattle the client, but the client has to stay calm, sensible and professional, and not answer it.

Steve Ellis

The media knows you won't speak when difficult negotiations are underway, or when a court case is pending, but the audience may not. The media needs pictures of you to wrap up their story. If they can get you to speak as well, all the better. What they're interested in is not *what* you say, but the *way* that you say it. The expression on your face will tell them as much as they need to know about your state of mind and how things are progressing.

Smile. Look confident. Appear vital. Notice how the US President George Bush *always* appears before the cameras striding, pointing, waving and speaking. The man would beam and make a speech about a sand dune in the desert. It means nothing, but it looks purposeful, alive and active.

Look as though the media circus are welcome guests rather than a besieging army, say nothing cheerfully, and move on. The electronic media prefers to shoot at a sitting target. A 'portable' ENG camera weighs 30lbs and some radio tape recorders can seem almost as heavy. So if you keep on the move, preferably towards a waiting car, they'll find it more than a little difficult to give chase.

It may be that you do feel in a position to give a short interview.

If so, you want your words picked up by as many people as possible. So the best way to avoid a media free-for-all, resulting in muffled sound bites and shots of your left ear poking out from behind a burly cameraman, is to organise the interviews into separate takes, say for BBC radio and TV and another for journalists in the Independent sector. If you've got time on your hands, take the radio interviews as a third separate group to avoid them crowding out the TV crews with their close-mike work.

But even if you do decide to make a bolt for it, don't resort to putting a plastic bag over your head like one senior figure from the Coal Board!

It's a Cover-up!

> When a Government department takes the trouble to send out a statement it often does so because there is something it is trying to hide... so look out for the wool being pulled over the eyes and never be afraid to ask an awkward question.
>
> Memo from national newspaper editor to his staff[18]

We've discussed a lot of ways to get out of a tight corner. And here's one that's worth repeating: never go into an interview hoping to pull off a cover-up. If you have a problem that's come to light and you've agreed to do an interview about it, the very best you can hope for is damage limitation, not deception. *Don't tell lies.* Even if you manage to draw a veil over the truth or throw the hounds off the scent, sooner or later the facts would be exposed, and you can be sure your words will be dredged up and used against you again and again. It's just not worth it.

And if the situation is utterly irredeemable...? What could be worse than being found guilty of causing 35 deaths through negligence and being fined a quarter of a million pounds? That's what happened to British Rail after a loose wire resulted in a train crash at Clapham Junction. BR's Chairman Sir Bob Reid took it on the chin. He said the BR Board had learned the lessons of Clapham:

> 'Everyone in the rail industry will always regret what has happened,' he told reporters outside the Old Bailey. 'We have pleaded guilty. Being here is a disgrace. We have to live with that, and we have to show in the future that this sort of thing cannot recur.,[19]

Admission, regret, the promise to do better next time. This man is saying he is accountable, he is responsible, he is sorry and he *cares.* Faced with such a display of penitence, who would begrudge him a second chance?

Strangely enough the ideal corporate interviewee would not be the polished performer. The absolutely ideal interviewee is somebody who is honest because he's giving honest answers. And that comes across. Somebody listening will say, 'Ah, he sounds to be an honest man.' The nice guy will come over best in the end.

Bud Evans

The media game is simply that. The stakes are high, but it is seldom, as in the example above, a matter of life and death. Bud Evans' 'nice guy' might be better conceived as the *sportsman* – the player who pours himself out in the fight to win, but whose step will still carry a spring whatever the outcome.

And that's not as trite as it may sound: the best way to preserve yourself and to acquire the psychological space essential to confidence, may be to regard the whole exercise as a sport; where what is at stake is not *yourself*, but the *game*. Like any professional player, you train, you practise, you plan, you go in hard and you *enjoy* it. If you win, celebrate, but if they lick you, you know you will walk away intact and bounce back next time.

TV is full of fragile egos. TV news is no exception. But any journalist who has achieved popular acclaim would acknowledge that even the hallowed news is simply a branch of a medium which has its roots in showbusiness, whose aim is to entertain.

Masterclass

Those are the principles, let's find out how practitioners from both sides of the divide put them into effect:

Jeremy Paxman, Newsnight

Ninety-nine per cent of interviews are just about eliciting information – that's all they are purely and simply. The confrontational interview is a very rare event and it is, by and large, confined to people in the political arena. It's most unusual that you find it going on elsewhere, so there's really nothing to fear.

180

Liz Howell, Managing Editor, Sky News

If you get a question that throws you and you don't know the answer, don't worry: just talk about something you *do* know about. The viewer would have to be very quick to realise that the question and answer didn't relate.

Don't panic, use simple language and if you know what you're talking about, you'll be alright. The best thing on television is a talking head saying the most interesting things – it's more riveting than any amount of gizmos and graphics.

A great example was an aircrash in the Midlands at Kegworth. [A Boeing 737 crashed onto the M1 killing 45]. Michael Bishop, the Chairman of British Midland Airways did a wonderful, probably unconscious PR job for himself, because he turned up, went on television and told it like it was. He was brilliant! If they're accessible and telt the truth as they understand it – it's unbeatable.

Michael Bishop, Chairman, British Midland Airways

It's old fashioned thinking to feel that the less you say, the less the matter will be reported.[20]

Alison Sergeant, BBC Radio Cambridgeshire

HOW DO YOU DEAL WITH BAD NEWS, SUCH AS STORIES OF REDUNDANCIES?

I would deal with them much more sympathetically if people would come clean with me. I don't like it when people give me a no-comment or refuse to talk to me. I see a challenge in this. A clever reporter wilt winkle out that information anyway. You can talk about natural wastage all you like, but when it comes down to job losses, it is much better to be honest and come out with a rational, sensible statement.

Businesses tend to blame outside forces for leading to redundancies, so I don't think any businessman needs to be afraid of handling a story like that in anything other than an honest and straightforward fashion.

What's more difficult is a story like a large chemical works where there has been an escape of gas or a mixture of chemicals or a spillage which has led to problems for the local community. On any number of occasions like that I have been met with a 'No comment, we are not at liberty to discuss this.'

There are other ways of finding out the information if the firm is not willing to tell us. We are very happy to go to the fire department, who I'm sure would tell us that the gases mixed together were X and Y. They might not attribute blame, but the implication might be clearly that gases X and Y ought not to have been stored together.

Had the firm come clean from the outset and said, 'This is what happened; this is what we have done in order to make the people in the area safe; this is what we are doing to make sure this sort of accident never happens again,' this would be a much brighter way of going about it than saying 'We are not at liberty to discuss it.'

HOW DO YOU THINK YOUR AUDIENCE VIEWS 'NO COMMENT?'

They think people have got something to hide.

SO YOU ARE SAYING IT IS BETTER TO LET THE TRUTH OUT BECAUSE IT GIVES YOU A CHANCE TO MITIGATE, RATHER THAN TRYING TO COVER IT UP, AS THE MEDIA WILL FIND OUT ANYWAY?

Absolutely. Reporters are inquisitive beasts, and if they have got wind of the story, they will go after it until they get some answers.

BUT SOMETIMES DIRTY QUESTIONS CAN BE SLIPPED IN. HOW SHOULD INTERVIEWEES DEAL WITH THOSE?

The cardinal rule is *never, ever,* lose your temper. You are not in control. you are not on your home territory, the interviewer is.

They also have ultimate control over the duration of the interview, so at the point you are about to launch into 'You

****** bastard', they can say 'Well, thank you very much, that's all we've got time for,' and straight into Dolly Parton. You're stumped. Nothing you can do. You will never get your viewpoint across. In 99 cases out of a hundred, you will be the loser if you lose your temper.

As for questions you simply don't know the answers to, they should have troubled to check their area of questioning, so you are not going to lose any Brownie points by saying 'I'm terribly sorry, I really don't have that information, I will have to come back to you.' In which case, do so.

WHAT IF YOU FIND YOURSELF TRAPPED – BEING QUESTIONED ABOUT SOMETHING SENSITIVE, TO WHICH YOU *DO* KNOW THE ANSWER BUT DON'T WISH TO GIVE IT?

There's is always some information you can give away. It might not be the full answer, but the chances are you can give them enough to persuade them to go away.

For example: you're going to make 20 per cent of your workforce redundant because of a management blunder which has led you into all sorts of financial problems. You have been terribly evasive throughout about coming clean about the fact that 20 per cent of your workforce is going to be fired. The interviewer knows perfectly well that this is the case, because he has actually had sight of a document communicating this information to the union. He's got an interview already in the can with the secretary of the Transport and General Workers, which is the union involved.

The biggest mistake you can make is being evasive. You can come clean perhaps about the redundancies, but hold back the reason for it being management incompetence. If you are very clever you can avoid the reasons for the redundancies.

YOU ARE TALKING ABOUT A SACRIFICIAL PAWN? EXPOSING A MINOR AREA OF WEAKNESS THAT WOULD BECOME THE TARGET OF ATTENTION?

Yes, I am.

WHAT YOU ARE DESCRIBING IS FINDING A WAY OF AMELIORATING BAD NEWS WITH THE OFFER OF SOMETHING MORE OPTIMISTIC IN THE FUTURE.

This requires a little bit of good management on your part before you reach the studio. For example: when glass was found in baby food, the manufacturers did two things. Firstly they withdrew all baby foods at risk from the market. Supermarket shelves were instantly emptied. And secondly, they were able to say at the interview at a very early stage that we are investigating ways of sealing so that this can never happen again. We will repackage to make sure that people cannot tamper with seals again.

SO IF BAD NEWS HAS BROKEN ABOUT YOUR COMPANY, GO IN WITH SOME GOOD NEWS TO SUGAR THE PILL?

If not some good news, then a responsible reaction: 'We are taking this very, very seriously. We don't make light of our mistakes, and we are doing A, B and C to put it right.'

FINALLY?

Simply identify the points you want to get across and make sure you do so. You can use the technique of saying 'That's an interesting point, however, the really *key* issue is...'

Somebody sat down and surveyed the numbers of questions answered by people very good at not answering questions. Mrs Thatcher came top. Neil Kinnock came second. So you too can play that game, providing you know the key points you want to get across, and you can dismiss the question that has been asked and put across the point that you want to make. But do it with courtesy, otherwise you will make someone very cross.

Steve Ellis, Media Counsellor, Burson-Marsteller (Public Relations Consultancy)

The media play on emotions as much as intellect – sometimes even more so. So in your response to any journalist across the media, you have to think of the emotional aspects as much as the intellectual. *How* you respond is as important as what you respond with.

We deal a lot with companies who are going through what they would term a crisis, where deaths have occurred, or have just been narrowly averted; where there have been mass redundancies, or an oilfield going up. And they have to say that they are very concerned.

Let's take an accident on an oil rig, where say 20 people have been killed in a helicopter crash. It's no use saying, 'Oh, we're very concerned about the loss of our workers...' They have to find a spokesperson who can say it and really *mean* it.

If the Chief Executive is such a hard-bitten sod that he just wants to get on with the business: '****! We're going to have to pay two million dollars in compensation!', then I would *not* recommend he goes on the media. If the media find *him*, that's one up for them.

First of all you have to accept the reality that the tragedy has happened. So no ostrich head in the sand stuff. Face it.

Secondly, say what you *can* say at the time – give information. It's not going to affect the legal situation if you're sorry. You can be humanly sorry; it doesn't necessarily mean admitting responsibility or liability, so you don't have to take all that rubbish that the lawyers tell you. The lawyers are the big problem in dealing with the media, because they're overcautious. In the long term it makes no difference.

Thirdly, say you are going to do something, as far as is humanly possible, to make sure whatever's happened is not going to happen again. Be reassuring as far as the future is concerned, that you will leave no stone unturned in finding out what's gone wrong.

So accept it's happened, be human in your response, and reassure them that you'll make sure as far as possible that it won't happen again.

Des Wilson, General Election Campaign Director, Liberal Democrats

WHAT CAN BE THE MOST TRAUMATIC THING ABOUT A TV INTERVIEW?

When you know you've screwed it up. I did an interview on Budget day, where I rushed over outside the House of Commons, did a quick spot, and I think I completely contradicted myself in the middle of it. With everything else going on, they didn't have the space to use it, but I spent the rest of the day completely apprehensive about what the Party would think of it when it appeared.

So no matter what experience you've had, you can still screw it up. The worst thing is waiting for it to come out. Often it's not as bad as you thought it was, but if it's recorded, and you're not happy with your performance, ask to do it again.

It's how you take command of a situation and how you negotiate the circumstances of it that's important. If there is an aggressive or difficult question, the person watching will prick up their ears and think, 'Hello, this is interesting.' But just by looking like you hear that question every day and have a complete answer to it, and by being totally calm about it, persuades the viewer that it isn't as serious as they thought – even if you haven't got a convincing answer.

Tony Benn, MP

When you get a question, whatever your view or qualifications, answer yes or no to begin with, otherwise you will earn a reputation for not answering questions. So say, 'No, but on the other hand...' or, 'Yes, but please remember...'

You have to make some pretence of answering the question but if you have got something you want to say, say it.

Try as hard as you can to think about the audience and not about the interviewer. Because the interviewer will very often dig a lot of little elephant traps, cover them in grass and edge you towards them, but you have to remember that the interviewer has a line of his own and it may not be the same as what you want to say.

186

HOW WOULD YOU PUT DOWN A JOURNALIST WHO YOU BELIEVE TO BE STUCK UP OR ARROGANT?

I don't think you should put anybody down, that would be a mistake, but sometimes a question is put which is offensive, and you could say, 'I think the spirit of that question could be rephrased, because what we are *really* talking about is...' and then you get it on to another point.

But of course, underlying it all is the argument about who sets the agenda. Is it to be set by elected people, or appointed people? And I have on occasions had to say to Robin Day – apart from 'Don't interrupt me...' – I have had to say, 'Now look, half a minute Robin, I have been elected and these are my views, and you've been appointed and these are *your* views.' Or alternatively, 'Is this an interview, or is this an argument?'

When they really decide to turn the flame-thrower on you, and I have had many, many occasions when they did, then you are in a defensive pose, and you have to do the best you can without sounding angry. I think it's terribly important never to get angry, and I never have. Keep very, very calm, but recognise that you may find yourself in what you thought was an interview, up against somebody whose apparent purpose is to destroy or undermine you, and then you have to protect yourself as best you can. You say, 'Look, I have agreed to come on because you wanted to talk about 'X', now you are seeking to turn it into something quite different.' And people on the whole understand that.

I get an awful lot of letters when I do have clashes, which I have had occasionally; people say, 'Thank God you said this to Robin Day,' or whoever it was, because you do get interviewers who try to dominate totally, and it annoys the listeners and the viewers quite as much as it may discomfort the person being interviewed.

If you are being shifty, people think you should answer that question and you won't. But if somebody presses you about the budget the day before the budget when the cabinet's been told but the country hasn't, you say, 'Well, look, I'm awfully sorry, but I can't deal with that because, as you will appreciate, tomorrow the statement's going to be made,' or 'Forgive me if I don't deal with that because the executive is meeting on Wednesday to discuss it,' or 'I don't want to deal with personalities.'

WHAT DO YOU DO IF IT ALL GOES WRONG?

You are moving now into an area which in some respects borders on trickery. I have had occasions when I have gone, thinking it was going to be one sort of a programme and discovering it was going to be another, or finding that questions are asked that I was assured I wouldn't be asked.

Very often the tape is still running, and you stop the interview, and you say, 'Well, you gave me an assurance that you wouldn't put the point.' Of course, as happened in the famous programme about Wilson, which was called 'Yesterday's Men', they went on filming while he protested, and they showed the film, which made him look utterly ridiculous. of course.

But there are occasions when you do just have to terminate an interview. And if it's a television interview, the best thing to do is to sit tight as though you haven't heard. They can't use something very easily where you haven't said anything. Better to do that actually, than to protest.

Charles Kennedy, Liberal Democrat MP

It is sometimes said that the relationship between the media and politicians is roughly akin to that which exists between a dog and a lamp post. [21]

What is not so clear is just who is the dog!

10

JUBILATION OR COMMISERATION?

Ed Koch was a real showman. He was very smart. He had lots of facts at his fingertips and he was terribly, terribly, entertaining. He really understood television... He was brilliant at the 30 second soundbite. Ed Koch always gives you a great quote.

The Media Show

Jubilation

Cashing in on Fame

First, let's be optimistic. You followed the gameplan, put your message across and went down well. You've chalked up thousands of pounds' worth of free publicity – why stop now when you're on a roll? You can cash in on your hard work and generate even more coverage. Lateral thinking and a good media directory can turn your appearance as newsmaker into yet more news that will make in local papers, trade journals and even the national press:

UNITED CHEMICALS CHIEF CALLS FOR TOUGHER POLLUTION LAWS

HEALTH UNION LEADER WARNS CUTS ARE ALREADY COSTING LIVES

300 NEW JOBS FOR GOSLING TRACTORS, AS CHIEF
EXECUTIVE UNVEILS EXPANSION PLANS

You will need to get the machine rolling well before your interview
goes out. News releases can be prepared on the wordprocessor, based
upon your message and angled towards the different media outlets.

When the interview is broadcast or published, quotes can be
transcribed from a recording and inserted into the text. Providing you
succeeded in getting your main point across – and that's the *whole
point*, isn't it – the process will be simple. Even if you didn't, or they
chose to highlight another comment, the news release can still lead
with your central message and be illustrated with whatever quote
they decided to use.

Fax or courier the end result for immediate distribution. Phone as
soon as is practicable to make sure it was received and brace yourself
to give another round of interviews! Then take a deep breath,
because you're not through yet!

If it's television get a video; if it's radio, get a cassette. Use it
as a promotional piece. First of all, send it throughout the
world to all the agencies one has, then, depending upon the
kind of business, send it out to customers and potential
customers. With a big engineering business it's justifiable and
it's possible. Next get a transcript and push that out to anyone
who's interested.

And you don't want to overlook the internal market –
employees are tickled pink to see their company on television
or radio.

Norman Hart, Managing Director Interact International Ltd

Learning from Experience

Now you can sit back and take stock. Every interview is a dress
rehearsal for the next one. Go through your recording closely,
watching for mannerisms, checking to see how your attitude came
across and considering ways to improve your performance. Order a
transcription of the interview so you can study a verbatim account of
what you said. See how closely you kept to your plan and whether

you got your message, your key points and your pointers across. If not, why not? Now's the time to check if you were adequately briefed and rehearsed and whether you need more training for the future.

To help you plot your performance over successive interviews, you might like to award yourself a system of points:

- 20 points for each key point you managed to put across. 10 points for each pointer.
- Give yourself a full 20 points for appearance, then deduct three points for each distracting mannerism, shifty look, or untidy item of clothing.
- Award yourself five points for each of the following indications of good attitude: credibility, warmth, enthusiasm, sincerity, alertness; and remove five points for each occasion when you came over as smug, insincere, aggressive, hesitant, ill-informed, foolish, etc.

If you can bear it, it's well worth asking someone else to check your performance and give you their unbiased verdict. But be careful- this can ruin a good working relationship!

Once you've started to consider how to give your best performance on air, you'll be amazed at how much more critical- or appreciative – you'll be of the on-screen performances of others. Interviews which would normally just wash over you will stand out with piercing clarity as models of how to – or how not to – perform on air. It's like buying a new car – you suddenly find that everyone else on the road has got the same model. Put your awareness to good use and watch to see how others perform, to see if you can pick up any tips – or offer any suggestions.

Commiseration

What if it still falls apart?

For all your careful preparation and caution, there will be times when the whole thing does blow up in your face and the media misrepresents you or distorts your argument, or worse. Any grievance is likely to fall into one of the following categories:

- abuse;
- distortion;
- errors; or
- lies.

Cases of genuine ill-treatment could be in breach of broadcasting guidelines. In the UK these cover both public sector and commercial broadcasters. Even Britain's national press covers that which should remain hidden behind a Code of Conduct (and with about as much effect as a fig-leaf...).

Distortion and errors can be corrected, and a complaint might just produce the desired result. Damaging statements might even be actionable. If there's any possibility that you've been libelled, take legal advice *immediately*. But if what it boils down to is that you took a harder pasting than you were expecting and came off a poor second, then your time and energy could be better used preparing more effectively for the next occasion. However, if you're convinced you're nursing a genuine grievance, then before you light the blue touch paper, first ask yourself two questions: 'Who, bar you and your colleagues would realise that a debacle has taken place? And what lasting harm has been done?'

By virtue of your expertise, you are on intimate terms with every nuance and subtlety of the issue. But the media has to reduce a subject to make it comprehensible to its audience in the time available. Unless you took steps to reduce it for them, as you should have done in your preparation, then some further reduction and distortion is inevitable.

Take check and be *reasonable*. It's better to win a friend than to defeat an enemy. Would an informal phone call to the reporter be more effective?

Broadcasting

If you really must do it by the book, first fire a shot across the bows. Prepare a succinct complaint and lodge it by phone immediately with the broadcasting company. Keep a copy and log the time of your call and the name of the recipient.

Before you engage in combat, you will need a transcript of the programme or segment in which your interview appeared. Unless you have a recording to hand, a transcript can be obtained from a monitoring company (see Appendix). Armed with the evidence, complain in writing to the named producer concerned and copy that to his or her immediate superior. Titles vary, so again, complain by name. Be specific, so your missive cannot be said to have gone missing in no-man's land.

Next, if you are still unsatisfied, escalate the action by writing directly to the producer's superior c.c. the station head or Director – again by name. Your next target is the regulatory body. In the UK, if your complaint concerns public sector radio or TV, write to the Director-General of the BBC. If the 'offence' has been committed by a commercial station, press your charge with the Independent Television Commission (for TV) or the Radio Authority. This is where the real authority lies. The ITC and the RA have the power to issue a reprimand, fine the company, shorten the term of its licence or revoke it entirely. Put your complaint in writing.

Your final barrage will be aimed at the Broadcasting Complaints Commission which considers allegations of unfair or unjust treatment by UK TV and radio in the commercial, BBC, satellite and cable sectors.

Complaints should be made by individuals or organisations with a direct interest in the issue and should be set out in writing. These are then sifted and weighed by the BCC's five commissioners who will direct the broadcasters to transmit a summary of the adjudication, even if it is not upheld. This is unlikely to carry the weight and prominence of the original item and the Commission is powerless to require them to publish an additional correction or apology, or to stump up a single penny in financial compensation.

So, after much effort, grim satisfaction would seem to be your best reward. Again, relevant addresses are given in the Appendix.

The Press

The UK press equivalent to the BCC is the Press Complaints Commission, which will consider complaints concerning privacy, the obtaining of information by subterfuge and the publication of factual errors. Once you have sent in your complaint with a copy of the offending item, the editor will be contacted. If there is no response or correction offered, the PCC would collect information from both parties and make an adjudication.

The newspaper has what the PCC describes as 'an unwritten obligation' to publish that adjudication. Due prominence is requested... As far as watchdogs go, the PCC, and the Press Council that preceded it, have all the deterrent value of an elderly Pekinese.

Libel

Being misrepresented by the media with its enthusiasm for distilling the meaning of life into a 15 second sound bite can be the rule rather than the exception. If pressure of space fails to distort the point, haste will often step in with a sprinkling of factual errors. Apart from bluster, there's little you can do. But if you consider yourself maligned to the degree that the audience or readership is likely to think significantly the worse of you, then you could be in another league altogether.

There is big money to be made from winning a libel suit – but heavy stakes to be paid out in costs if you lose – and sometimes if you win. And the process is horrendously time-consuming and hardly likely to endear you to the media in the future. You may have a case if what has been said about you is factually wrong and capable of damaging your reputation, or if a damaging opinion has been expressed which is malicious or based on incorrect information. Of course there's more to it than that. That's why lawyers drive BMWs. Stump up for legal advice immediately.

Biting the Bullet

Frankly, if your grievance is not actionable, then your best bet is to simply bite on the bullet or try for a swift correction or apology – for what it's worth. And whatever that comes to, console yourself, the sum will be nowhere near the value of all that free peak-time publicity the media gave you in the days when things did work out – or could give you in the future.

Once there's been a debacle on screen, there's little you can do beyond binding up your injured and burying your dead. A more effective use of resources could be to invest in training and preparation for the future.

Masterclass

Des Wilson, Liberal Democrat General Election Campaign Director

IF AN INTERVIEWEE HAS BEEN BADLY TREATED, WHAT KIND OF COMEBACK IS THERE?

Virtually none, and there's no point usually in bothering to try, because you can't win. Television people are incredibly good at defending themselves, and claiming that they were right. I've never heard a television person admit they were wrong about *anything*.

You've got to learn the lesson and look after yourself. It's a hard world we live in and it really is no good grouching and saying, 'I'm inexperienced and I didn't know they were going to do that.'

There's hardly a day goes by where one isn't annoyed about the media, but I've learned there usually isn't a lot of point in complaining. Learn from experience, avoid it happening and next time be more careful and tough about it.

11

TRAINING

You can read a million books about how to handle the TV interview; until you go into the studio environment and have a few spotlights on you and a couple of cameras up your nose, a microphone pinned to your tie and someone looking your straight in the eye it's the difference between reading a language and talking it. And you can't get any feedback from a book.

Steve Ellis

The Wheat from the Chaff

Say you'd never driven before, what organisation would hand you the keys to a company car and leave you to get on with it? And what kind of fool would you be to accept? The inevitable mistakes and mishaps or worse would be damaging and public – to both parties. And for television appearances, worth a small company's turnover in publicity, the stakes are too high to leave it to chance.

Media training courses abound, and are variable – both in cost and quality. They range from the cheap and cheerful, put on by a local college with a TV unit, to the glossy, corporate and costly. Price is not necessarily indicative of worth. The key considerations are:

- How much time will you personally spend putting the theory into practice?
- And is your tutor speaking from experience?

11. Training

At the very least, a media training session should offer you several cracks at being interviewed and give you personal, constructive, specific feedback.

There are three stages. First screening – you chuck all sorts of questions at them and they make all kinds of a muck of it. Then you do an inquest on that; you run back the video and you look at it; then you do it again.
Norman Hart, Managing Director, Interact International Ltd

If you have yet to experience a television interview, you will need to be put through your paces under the heat and the lights of a proper television studio. A video camera and a single lamp is a poor substitute for your baptism of fire. Unless your organisation has its own studio your training will take place off site and will require the hiring of a studio and facilities, camera operators and a director. Three or four cameras are standard fare, and allow authentic shot changes to be made between you and your interviewer, as well as those tell-tale close-ups. It's expensive.

Companies often seem to assume that a single session will crack it. It should soften the fear of the unknown, but a total of ten minutes under a lamp and in front of a lens will not produce a polished performer. Sessions, such as my own, offer personal, detailed and specific feedback on your appearance, your performance (delivery) and your message. Next you will need time to assimilate that advice, adjust your appearance, practise and polish your performance and hone your message to perfection. Then it's back to the studio. Partial success can be achieved in a single session, with a limited number of candidates. But to reinforce soundly, the session should be repeated the following day, or as soon as is practicable. Top-up sessions should be held at least once a year. The CBI runs training courses four times a year.

Exercises should replicate the range of media realities. As a minimum, as well as the studio interview there should be location interviews for both TV and radio. To create simulations that are as realistic – and therefore as useful – as possible, you should be working from authentic news releases, and your trainers should be able to present you with the results of your interview as they would appear in the press or on radio. To produce an edited TV location report would require additional interviews and location shots –

possible, but complex, time-consuming, technology-dependent and therefore even more expensive. Again, for authenticity, your trainers should be given copies of your news releases well in advance of the session in order to be able to research the subject and prepare an interview.

At the bespoke end of media training are the organisations that will come out at short notice to rehearse you on the spot for an imminent TV appearance. They will help you construct your message and tailor it to suit the styles and individual requirements of different audiences. They can play devil's advocate and test your argument for any weaknesses and will advise you on your presentation.

> I appreciate that in live interviews people can be somewhat thrown by the circumstances, but since it is essentially a conversation, I think once you've done it once or twice you just get used to the convention, and anybody who's been on a media training course will understand what's involved.
>
> Jeremy Paxman

The Screentest

The training session can also be an invaluable filter to screen out poor performers who would not enhance a company's standing. Cameras do peculiar things to appearance, and adrenalin can play havoc with composure. Many will pass with flying colours, but a minority will fail spectacularly – and in a way that cannot be predicted until you see them on the screen, as media counsellor Steve Ellis explains:

> The more I train people for TV, the more I believe in the Hollywood screentest. There are some faces and some voices, however honest, credible and sincere, that somehow just don't come across on TV and radio as being so.
>
> There's a little game I play every time I go to a media training session. I predict which one will *look* good on TV; which one will *sound* good and which ones *won't*.
>
> Most of my predictions are wrong. That's why even big Hollywood directors still have screen tests for potential movie

stars. Because until you actually see them, there is something about people going from three dimensions to the two. Some qualities just come through.

You see one guy and you think, 'He's overweight, he's going bald, his specs are funny,' and then you see him on TV and he's *believable*. And then you get some big guy: six foot two, square jaw, big eyes and you think, 'He'll go well on TV,' but when you put him on screen he looks shifty, like a poor second-hand car salesman. There's no way you can tell.

There are others who are competent, but just can't cope with the camera in front of them. They start shaking and get very nervous. That's why training is necessary in the first place.

As you can imagine, training sessions produce the most marvellous blackmail material! There's a more serious point here. It is vital to select individuals and organisations whose confidentiality you can rely upon. If you are to strengthen your weaknesses, you will need to expose the areas in which you are most vulnerable to your trainer or consultant, who will then be able to target them specifically and rehearse you for any eventuality.

False Economy?

The closer you get to the real thing, the more valuable, and more costly, the exercise becomes. But let's put it in perspective. A single 30 second advertisement during the commercial break of *News at Ten* could cost you £27,000. And that is for the Thames region alone. The fourteen other ITV regions also take *News at Ten* and also charge for advertising. A typical news report on the programme will extend to three or four times the length of that single 30 second advert.

Eight million people will be watching the item on *News at Ten*. Versions of that item may also appear on other ITN news summaries. Their combined audience will be well in excess of the combined circulation of every British national daily newspaper. And the story itself is likely to be picked up and used extensively by the rest of the media – if they haven't already covered it. So what price a convincing, authoritative and effective interview on primetime news? And how much more credible would that be than an advert? Media training can be expensive. But what is it worth to insure against fouling up, putting your foot in it, or blowing the opportunity through being inexperienced, ill-prepared and under-rehearsed?

Masterclass

John Pike, Manager Media Affairs, Shell UK

Skilled interviewers are doing it day in day out and we are are just visitors to it a few times in our lives. Although we learn all the time, we are never going to be as good as they are unless we do it almost daily. The idea that you have television and radio training once in your life is just nonsense. You've really got to do it certainly every year. We put our people through radio and television training regularly. It's not like circumcision, done once and never again. The more you do it, the more confident you become.

Bud Evans, an Editor of the Today *programme*

It was during a training session with spokesmen for a public utility. One complaint had been that too many people were being cut off because they weren't paying their bills. The company's case was that they went through elaborate procedures before cut-off could occur. But in the hypothetical case, the woman had not received any warnings. Somebody arrived to cut her off. She wasn't in so they broke the door down. The woman claimed compensation.

In the course of the interview I asked the spokesman, 'How do you feel *personally* about this?' He went on to explain the official company policy, and I said to him, 'Now put yourself in the position of the woman, the way she must have reacted to find her home broken into...' And he began to look at it from her point of view.

As I continued to press him, not only did he say the policy was totally *wrong*, but in the same group on his media training day was his immediate boss, who was not at all amused! He shouldn't have been drawn into personal hypothesis.

Normal Hart, Managing Director, Interact International Ltd.

There are all manner of hang-ups. I reckon the worst, which is not unknown, is that the speaker dries up completely. They'll shed a tear or two, and do all manner of atypical things.

HOW DO YOU IRON THAT OUT?

Oh, just switch the camera off and have a little heart-to-heart talk, and then you switch it back on again, and it's lovely. That's why they do the practice in the first place.

Tony Benn, MP

Take trades unionists against businessmen. Because they are more democratic in the sense that they have to be elected to shop' steward, area council, national executive; on the whole they are much more articulate than businessmen, who are appointed.

You can always tell somebody who is not familiar with the process of arguing their case, they are stiff, they are formal, whereas the people who are used to arguing are very plain; they say, 'Look, let's get this straight; the key thing here is this...'

But I'm very, very sceptical of all the media training arguments, beyond that fact that you go to a studio and somebody fires a lot of questions at you and you think, 'Now, how the hell should I deal with *that* if it came up?' In that sense rehearsal may be useful.

Andrew Clayton, Editor, Business Daily, *Channel 4*

There are good and bad training courses. A lot of guff can be taught. Sometimes training courses have made people too 'pally'. I've heard of people telling trainees to use the interviewer's Christian name. There shouldn't be a 'pallyness' between them if it doesn't exist. It has a bad effect on the audience; they don't like it and it makes the whole thing artificial.

Insofar as training allows people to come across a film crew or the studio – the hardware of a TV interview – before they have to do it in earnest, it's a good idea. And if it makes people direct and sensible, and answer the question put to them, it's a good thing.

Liz Howell, Managing Editor, Sky News

A lot of these bad courses that were set up in the 19805 told people to take the interview out of the interviewer's hands and turn to the camera and address it. That completely ***** up your eyelines and everything. They *mustn't* do that. You must look at the interviewer and respond to the interviewer, because it's more effective. They're not trying to make you look stupid. But a lot of business people who'd been on courses completely ruined the interviews by looking into the camera.

The worst thing is if they speak at the same time as the interviewer through sheer nerves; that's terribly irritating.

Steve Ellis, Media Counsellor Burson-Marsteller (Public Relations Consultancy)

No-one is too good not to need media training. There are very senior politicians who every time before they go on *Question Time* go and warm up round the table with three or four journalist friends who fire questions at them and get them up to speed.

I can think of at least three Cabinet members who *need* to go back to school to learn how we do it today.

I've run sessions for the Budget where we simulate a live studio session with news coming as the budget's unveiled, and then I go to people around the table and ask them for their reactions. When they go over in the afternoon to the real TV studio, they're up to speed.

It's the actual experience, as opposed to theory; the practice of being interviewed and firing back responses to live questions.

ARE THERE SOME THINGS YOU CAN'T PREPARE FOR?

I worked on the *Herald of Free Enterprise*, Bhopal and Heysel Stadium stories as a reporter. And there's nothing that can prepare a chief executive to be in a room with half a dozen cameras, dozens of microphones and tape recorders on the table and reporters from *The Sun, News of the World* and *National Enquirer* spitting at you as soon as you walk out from your quiet office. *That* you have to experience.

WHAT'S THE WORST GAFFE AN INEXPERIENCED INTERVIEWEE COULD MAKE, AND HOW COULD TRAINING HELP THEM AVOID IT?

The worst mistake they could make would be a lack of preparation and the arrogance to think they don't need it. They have two or three minutes on air and come away thinking, 'Oh UU, I didn't really want to say that', or 'Oh, they've edited that badly', and what they've done is to throw away hundreds of thousands of pounds' worth of a media opportunity to really get their message home. Not only that, but if they're no good on TV or radio, producers will be very reluctant to ask them back.

APPENDIX I:

BRIEFINGS

---

1 How to Grab them by the Ears

- Be pro-active, positive and promote.

- News is whatever *impacts* on a given audience.
  - It has to be relevant.
  - The marketability of news will depend on the scale and strength of its impact.

- Tailor your news to suit the market – and promote it.

- Media feeds off media. Once one makes a show of it, others will want it.

Generating News

- News can be *generated* as well as discovered.
  - The media is interested in conflict and controversy.
  - Your reaction may be welcomed on a current issue, provided you are an acknowledged expert or bona-fide spokesperson.
  - Practical responses to current events are newsworthy, especially if they engage the emotions.

Softer Stories

- The regional media and the tabloid press thrives on human interest items.

- Stories about people can be newsworthy if they are presented in an appealing way. Try to:
  - capture the public imagination; and
  - aim for visual impact.

Targeting the Media

- If you are too busy to generate and market your own news you may need to enlist a PR company.

- The campaign will be to:
  - determine your audience
  - find suitable media outlets; and
  - track down the right contact.

- Your audience will be international, national, regional, local, or special interest, or a combination of these.

- Outlets will be TV, radio, newspapers, magazines, trade press, teletext, etc.
  - Precisely target your contacts in each.
  - Commercial media listings give up-to-date details of contacts.

- Adapt your message to the different markets.

Delivering Your Message

- Select the best way of bringing your message to the medium – news release, news conference, news briefing or personal contact.

- Personal contact is crucial.

News Conference

- For large, set-piece launches and announcements:
  - have them arranged by an expert;
  - choose a date and a time to suit media deadlines; and

- – offer broadcasters individual interviews, preferably in advance, under embargo.

- Media contact on a less formal, smaller-scale is often preferable.

News Briefings and Facility Visits

- Target a few key contacts for a discussion over lunch or breakfast. They should be representative of a spread of the media.

- Consider offering a facility visit to get acquainted with the media. Peg it to a news announcement which you will make during the visit.

- Facilities need careful planning, including knowledgeable escorts, food, accommodation where necessary, and a press room.

The News Release

- Usually the prime point of contact with the media.

- Releases are:

  - – generally binned with scarcely a second glance; and
  - – usually badly targeted and badly written.

- The release should:
  - – be adapted to different audiences;
  - – be customised for the quality, trade and consumer press and the local media;
  - – point up the relevance to the individual audience; and
  - – highlight the news angle *immediately* in the headline and the introduction.

- Your message has five seconds to connect.

- Your news release should arrive at least five working days before the event – otherwise fax it. If it's urgent and imminent, fax and phone.

- However good your story, stronger items may still squeeze you off the schedule.

News Pictures

- A good picture may give prominence to your item.

- Go for lively, interesting and attention-grabbing shots.

- Avoid posed and stilted mugshots.

- Consider building up a portfolio.

Embargoes

- Embargoes place a release date and time on a story, which you are requesting the media to observe. There is little you can do if they ignore it.

- Choose your embargo date and time to best suit the various publication deadlines of your target media.

- Make sure the embargo is blindingly obvious.
  - Loom it large at the top of the news release.
  - Remind them of it when they are arranging the interview.
  - Get their agreement to abide by it before you go further

- Embargo only major stories.
  - This gives the media time to arrange background coverage
  - And can give you the space to spread your attention.
  - Don't try to embargo running stories – they'll get the information from another source and run it anyway, embargoed or not.

Deadlines

- Once you have targeted your media find out their deadlines and work within them.

Building up Contacts

- Know and be known.

- Target specialists in your field
  - And decision makers such as editors, news editors and producers.
  - Don't neglect TV researchers for relevant programmes.

- Establish a relationship with a reputable news agency which will develop your story and market it to other media outlets.

- If you have several contacts under one roof, contact them individually.

- Cultivate contacts. Wine them and dine them once a year.

- Keep your list up-to-date.

2 Should you give the interview

- Fear of the unknown is often the real reason for refusing.

- But the benefits of accepting could include:
  - raising your organisation's profile;
  - promoting the interests of your cause;
  - enhancing your company's image;
  - valuable and extensive free publicity; and
  - the chance to get your organisation out of a tight corner plus a boost to your own career prospects.

- And if you don't take advantage of the opportunity, your rivals might.

- Before you agree you will need to find out the angle – this is the perspective the report is taking on the story.

Pre-interview Checklist

- Weigh up the motives and purpose of the caller to judge whether the interview would be in your interest.

- Record your preliminary phone conversation with the producer.

- Your aim is to find out whether what *they* want to hear matches what *you* want to say. Put yourself in their shoes – what would *you* ask?

- Use the CHECKLIST on pages 32-34 to find out:
  - the purpose of the interview;
  - the ground to be covered;
  - the motive behind it;
  - the programme or publication it's for;
  - the interviewer who'll conduct it (you need to know if he or she is a specialist);
  - when and where it'll take place (in a studio or on location);
  - whether it'll be live or pre-recorded;
  - the source of the story – if you haven't seen the original ask them to fax it;
  - who else will appear in the report, and whether you can preview their comments – also ask to preview any accompanying material;
  - find out the time and date of transmission/publication; and
  - get as clear an idea as possible about the line of questions.

- Don't commit yourself to the interview until you are satisfied about their intentions.

- Basic interview questions are:
  - What's happening now?
  - What's new?
  - How will it affect the audience?
  - What's the scale of it?
  - What are its advantages/disadvantages?
  - And what happens next?

- If you see a problem, do the consequences of refusing the interview outweigh the benefits of accepting?
  - Be more disposed to accept than to refuse.
  - Bad news can usually be turned to good publicity
  - Saying nothing could cause more damage.

- If the interview is for future publication, will the facts still hold true?
  - If not, press to do it at a later date.
  - If in doubt think it over then ring back within 20 minutes.

- Be available.

- Be flexible.

- Consider subscribing to a cuttings service.

- Familiarise yourself with the different programmes and media outlets that might call on you for an interview.

Who Should Do It?

- The ideal interviewee:
  - has expert knowledge;
  - is a good communicator;
  - is an experienced on-air performer;
  - has an attractive personality;
  - a clear and lively voice;
  - for TV, should be easy on the eye; and
  - is available.

- Select potential TV performers by purring them through a screen test to judge.

Live or Recorded?

- Live interviews are not edited, so what you say is what goes out.
  - But they can be more disruptive of your time, and are subject to cancellation.
  - Recorded interviews are subject to selection and may be packaged in a less favourable context.

If in Doubt...

- If you have to turn them down:
  - make sure they understand why; and
  - keep an open door for the future.

3 Preparing the Interview

- Preparation is vital. You are about to address an audience of thousands, possibly millions. Plan what you want to say, and how you intend to say it.

The Message

- If your interviewer is following up a news release he/she will want to take the information further.
- He/she will want to know the story's:
  - significance;
  - implications;
  - problems; and
  - what will happen next.

- He/she will play devil's advocate to test for weaknesses. Anticipate the line of questioning by putting yourself in their shoes.

- Check the company line before you plan your response.

- Aim to leave one clear impression which has impact – your message. It should be:
  - short;
  - relevant;
  - simple;
  - crystal clear;
  - have impact; and
  - be memorable.

- Use pointed phrases that capture the imagination. After the interview anyone in the audience should be able to sum up the point in a single sentence. And that sentence should match your message.

- Begin with your conclusion then introduce evidence that will prove your point.

211

- Tailor your message to match the journalist's perception of the story. If *you* don't, *he* will.

- Don't prepare too much material.

Key Points and Pointers

- Divide your argument into two or three key points – no more.
  - Each should make a positive statement.
  - For each key point produce two or three supporting pointers.
  - You should be able to state each point and pointer in a single sentence.

- In a short interview get your main point across *immediately.*

- Keep your material lean. Avoid qualifying your argument – qualifications are likely to be edited out.

What's in it for me?

- Every interview must have a 'what's in it for me' angle. This is a golden thread which appeals to and benefits the audience. That thread should run through each key point until they combine to form your message.

- If you're given more time, don't *add* to the information, *reinforce* it.

Making Notes

- Use notes as a safety net and *aide memoire* only
  - Keep them out of sight of the camera.
  - Make them clear.
  - Write them as prompts you can recognise at a glance on a single file-card (for TV).
  - Only glance down to look at them when the camera is likely to be *off* you, and/or when you are being asked questions.

Anticipate Difficult Questions

- Recognise contentious points

- Rehearse how you'll deal with them. Get a colleague to play devil's advocate.

- Produce answers that will counter the argument, reassure your audience, and promote your company.

Rehearsal

- Rehearse your material well but don't learn it off by heart – allow for some spontaneity.

- Learn the *facts*, not the script.

- Know your key points and pointers – and practise putting them across.

Assume no Prior Knowledge

- Always address yourself to the layman.

Avoid Jargon

- Don't hide yourself or your message behind jargon.

- Translate *everything* into plain English.

- Keep it simple, but don't patronise and beware of oversimplifying to the point of becoming inaccurate.

Simplify Figures

- Round them up or down

- Use only one or, at most, two.

- Avoid fractions.

- Never use decimals.

Explain Abstract Ideas

- Use metaphors and analogies to help people to *see* what you mean:
  - 'It's like this...'
  - Always bring ideas down to a human level.

Use Anecdotes

- Pointed stories about *people* give your argument a human angle. Use *one* as support only, and keep it crisp.

Supplying Graphics

- Graphics can make your point more effectively than words. Consider:
  - drawings;
  - large photos;
  - slides; and
  - a corporate video.

- Discuss content and format with the producer – quality is paramount.

- The media may wish to adapt your material to their house style.

Promote the Company Name

- Be careful with plugs:
  - One mention only is typical.
  - The media may do it for you.
  - Discuss it with the producer.
  - Overdo it and it could be your last appearance.

Foreign Language Interviews

- Don't attempt the lingo unless you speak it fluently.

- Ask them to interview you in English – most times they will be able to.

- If they won't, delegate the task.

- As a last resort, use an interpreter.

Foreign Perspectives

- To tailor your news message to a foreign audience you will need to understand their news agenda.

- An international cuttings service may help.

- Consider the services of a consultant. Some still regard UK news interviewing as tougher than in the rest of Europe.

4 The Television Interview

Getting There

- Check *which* studio to go to and who to ask for when you arrive.

- Ask them to send a car if transport is a problem. In any event, don't drive yourself.

- Get there early – and ask to be shown round the studio to demystify it.

Hospitality – Beware!

- Keep your own counsel in hospitality.

- Regard everything you say as on-the-record.

- Avoid sweet or milky drinks.

- Avoid alcohol.

- Let your adrenalin work for you. If you need to, unwind beforehand by stretching and deep breathing.

Just Checking

- Check that the following are as you expected:
  - the interviewer;
  - co-interviewees; and
  - the area of questioning.

- If changes leave you at a serious disadvantage, protest. As a last resort, refuse to go on air.

- Ask for an idea of the first question.

- Ask to see the introduction.

- Find out whether a taped report will accompany the interview.
  - Ask to preview it. (This is not your right.)
  - Failing that, ask for details of contents and speakers.

- Check the length of the interview.

Setting up

- Let them fit you with a microphone.
  - Sit and speak for the sound check as you would in the interview.
  - *Always* be discreet near a microphone – the control room can hear every word and NEVER swear near a mike.

- The floor manager will signal to the interviewer.

- The presenter has to listen to instructions through an earpiece so their attention is divided.

- Live interviews can be shifted or cut to make way for breaking news.

Remote Studios

- These usually contain a single remote-controlled camera.

- Eye contact is lost with the interviewer but:
  - act and react as though you *do* have eye contact throughout;
  - respond to the camera lens as though it were your interviewer's face; and
  - keep the performance going, as you never know when the camera will be on you.

- The director will tell you which way to look to give the impression that you are facing one another.

- You'll be given an earpiece so you can hear the questions – wear it in the ear turned from the camera.

- Remote interviews require greater concentration.

Location Interviews

- These offer greater visual interest by providing shots to illustrate the story.

- Be selective about where the cameras should go:
  - steer them towards a suitable backdrop prepared in advance that would show your organisation to advantage;
  - clean up beforehand, if necessary;
  - look for a location offering strong natural light;
  - for desk shots, arrange your office to convey busy efficiency;
  - get the company name in view;
  - for home or office shots, get bookshelves in the background;
  - if they want to pick their own locations, brief a polite minder to steer them clear of trouble spots; and
  - don't be bullied into being interviewed in inappropriate locations or circumstances – they *need* your cooperation.

- For shooting out of doors keep hairspray handy.

Pre-chat

- Establish rapport with the interviewer.

- Check the line of questions, and offer any additional information.

- Ask in advance if you can retake any answers you are unhappy with.

Shooting the Location Report

- The crew of two or three and the reporter will often arrive separately.
  - The crew may not be well briefed about the story.
  - Show them where they should go.
  - Win their favour by showing hospitality.
  - If they take a disliking to you they can make you look *awful.*

The Shots

- Most recorded interviews are conducted with a single camera.
  - The camera operator will shoot an establishing shot, and then concentrate on your answers.
  - Afterwards reaction shots will be taken of the reporter nodding and any insert shots of objects or actions. These will be used to mask the eventual edits in your interview.
  - The reporter may then be recorded asking his questions on camera. Stay to make sure any revised questions are still fair to you.

Record it Yourself

- Make your own recording so you can compare the original interview with the edited version.

When will it go out?

- News items are subject to rescheduling.
  - Don't rely on them to tell you when it will go out.
  - Call them to check, but record successive programmes just in case.

Actuality Interviews

- Verité, or slice of life reports, feature *you*, but no reporter.

- You'll need to speak in statements, rather than answers, so the reporter's questions can be cut out.

- If they film you at work, act naturally – but *always* remember you're on camera.

5 The Radio Interview

- Radio's appetite for news is enormous.

- Local radio allows you to *personally* address your own clients and constituents.

- It is usually faster, simpler and more accessible than TV – fewer people are involved in the production process.

- Reports follow a similar format to TV – they need short, quotable quotes to illustrate a news bulletin, or two or three minute interviews.

- Interviews take place on location, in the studio, remote studio, radio car, or over the phone; live or pre-recorded.

- Radio is often more immediate than TV and will press you to act quickly – but take time to run the pre-interview checklist before agreeing to the interview.

- General news reporters in local radio will seldom have time to research a story – be prepared to fill in the background details.

- Local radio values its contacts – but be prepared for tough questions if the subject is controversial.

The Recorded Interview

- Location interviews are conducted by a solo reporter with a portable recorder.

Setting up

- Sound quality is critical.
  - The interview room should be noise and echo-free – ideally small and well-draped with soft furnishings.
  - Anticipate distractions – unplug the phone; prevent interruptions; shut off noises.
  - Be prepared to move to another location if necessary – go out of doors as a last resort.

- The reporter will need to get close to you to interview you.
  - Come out from behind your desk.
  - The ideal recording position is knee-to-knee, close enough for the microphone to pick up both of you.
  - Don't be intimidated by the proximity of the mike -look beyond it to keep eye contact with the reporter.

- Find out the length the item will run to and tailor your message to fill. They will be grateful if they don't need to edit you.

Sound Effects

- Radio reports use sound effects as TV uses pictures. If your location produces appropriate sounds offer to take the reporter to record them.

The Phono

- Radio news will require interviews recorded on the telephone. These are brief and immediate, and you may be pressed to record an interview immediately.

- Ask for time to prepare but be mindful of their deadlines.

- They may need to call you back to get a good phone-line and sufficient volume – never bellow to be heard.

- If you are giving a live interview make sure your own radio is turned off to avoid feedback.

- They should never record you over the phone without your permission.

The Radio Studio

- Before you go in, check the name of the programme and your interviewer.

- Be familiar with the style of the programme – if there's time listen to it yourself – or ask the producer to send you a tape.

- The presenter will usually be given a list of questions by the producer and be directed during the interview. Check beforehand with the producer how you will be introduced and the area of questioning.

- The studio equipment will be operated by a studio manager or by the presenter himself. If the programme is self-operated the presenter is likely to be distracted during the interview.

- Check whether excerpts may be taken from your interview for use in news bulletins.

- Radio will seldom pay your expenses to go into the studio!

Phone-ins

- Never allow yourself to be pressed to appear at short notice on a live discussion programme or phone-in. There is less control over

221

questions from the audience, and more preparation is necessary to anticipate possible questions.

Microphone Discipline

- Stay between 15 and 50cm from the mike.

- Don't:
  - shift your position after the soundcheck;
  - wear a coat that rustles and beads that rattle;
  - click your biro;
  - drum fingers;
  - thump the table;
  - kick the mike stand; or
  - use large sheets of paper that can brush the mike or drag on the desk.

- You may be asked to wear headphones – ask them to adjust the volume until it is comfortable.

- When the red studio light comes on, you are on air.

The Remote Studio

- Radio stations often have remote studios in places such as county hall.
  - They save going out to the radio station.
  - They can be small, bare and intimidating.
  - There will usually be someone on hand to help you operate it.
  - Eye contact is lost yet some interviewees prefer the absence of distractions.

The Radio Car

- This is a mobile studio to cover breaking stories.

- If you are important enough or immobile enough they may send the car to you rather than require you to go in.

- Eye contact is lost and it is harder to take part in a discussion.

Your Voice

- Be bright, lively, positive and confident and seek to establish rapport with one imaginary listener.

- Radio favours rich voices.
  - Use yours to the full, by making your mouth, your lungs and your larynx work.
  - But beware of losing your naturalness.
  - Practise into a tape recorder.

A Happy Medium

- Radio is an ideal training ground for broadcast interviews.

- Make contact with senior management from both news and programming (news editor and programme controller or programme organiser).

- Promote yourself across both departments of the radio station.

- Local radio identifies with and affirms its audience and the area they live in. If you do too you are likely to prove popular.

6 Newspaper and Magazine Interviews

- Newspaper and magazine interviews hold fewer technological terrors than those for broadcasting.

- Most interview requests will be for brief quotes over the phone, though feature articles will require longer face-to-face interviews.

- Before you give the interview:
  - run through the usual checklist;
  - find out also if the interview is for a news item or a feature;
  - find out how much they need to know about *you*;
  - find out how *long* the piece will run to;
  - find out *who* is going to interview you;
  - familiarise yourself with their work and their publication so you can gauge their likely approach and political position;

223

- ascertain their deadlines – understand the pressure they are under and accommodate it; and
- find out the publication date and adjust your message to be appropriate *then* – magazine lead times can be lengthy.

Distortion

- The more you say, the more selective they can be. So:
  - Stick to your message; and
  - amplify it rather than add to it.

- Note-taking will be either by cassette recorder or shorthand. As usual, keep a recording yourself to minimise the likelihood of distortion. Do it openly, but discreetly, to avoid comment.

- Beware the interviewer who does all the talking. You could end up reading his opinions rather than your own.

- Don't insult a journalist by asking him/her to show you the copy before it is published. Unless the power of veto is *vital*, then negotiate it while the interview is being arranged.

- If facts change before the interview is published, inform the journalist *immediately*. The later you leave it the more disruptive your changes become, and if the publication has gone to press, you will be too late.

Don't be seduced

- Print interviews can be more convivial than those for broadcasting but don't let your guard slip.

- Regard *every* conversation with a journalist as on-the-record unless you both agree otherwise.

- The absence of a notebook or recorder means nothing.

Strong-arm Tactics

- The local press is less likely to give you a hard time. But if they do:
  - don't threaten to withdraw your account.
    Advertising and editorial are usually kept separate;
  - plough your energy into preparing a good interview.

Press Pictures

- Prepare interesting and appropriate locations beforehand.

- Beware candid camera shots
  - Pictures of you looking strained or troubled could be used at a later date.
  - Ask beforehand for the right of veto of all picture negatives, or only agree to give posed shots or have your *own* shots taken.

- Consider preparing a portfolio of good pictures. Go for:
  - variety, interest, action and lively backdrops;
  - a combination of people and hardware; and
  - avoid shoulder-by-shoulder pictures.

- A good shot will increase the prospect of publication – and grab column inches.

Graphics

- Newspapers and magazines appreciate good graphics. They are more likely to run unchanged in print than on TV.

- Graphics add visual appeal and eliminate turgid explanations.

- They may increase the chances of a story being used and increase the space available to it

7 Putting Yourself Across

How you Look

- TV is a medium of first impressions, so take special care over your appearance.

- Be smart:
  - Dress to look confident, credible and authoritative.
  - Dress conservatively, as you would for a job interview.
  - Pick a tie that complements your shirt.

- Avoid:
  - small checks;
  - stripes;
  - bright white;
  - brown;
  - swathes of brilliant colour;
  - bare arms;
  - off-the-shoulder dresses;
  - photochromatic glasses;
  - bright jewellery;
  - large earrings; and
  - badges and motifs.

- Go for a dark, but positive colour like navy.

- Carry nothing in your pockets.

- Button your jacket.

- Smooth your jacket line by sitting on its tail.

- Women prone to neck flushes should wear a scarf.

- Check with the producer before you dress for the interview.

- Men and women should use light make-up. If they offer to make you up, accept. If you think you need it, ask for it.

226

- Don't smoke.

- Go to the loo before your interview – check your appearance while you're there:

  - carry a pocket mirror;
  - tidy your hair front and back,
  - brush your hair away from your eyebrows; and
  - check your tie is straight and firmly knotted.

How you Seem

- The television interview is a performance. To come over well you will need to be larger than life, without seeming hyper. Aim for:

  - confidence;
  - credibility;
  - warmth;
  - sincerity; and
  - enthusiasm.

- Project yourself as:

  - lively;
  - vital;
  - alert;
  - compelling;
  - relevant;
  - inspiring;
  - human; and
  - when appropriate, amusing.

- Avoid:

  - arrogance;
  - pomposity;
  - self-importance;
  - insincerity;
  - trying too hard to please; and
  - vanity.
  - But don't be too modest!

- Beware of reflecting back the mood of your interviewer if he is dour or sceptical – project your own persona and try to lift the atmosphere.

- Never act as though you were addressing a mass audience – speak to one person.

Are you Sitting Comfortably...?

- Sit comfortably in your seat and lean slightly forward.

- Avoid:
  - shifting around;
  - crossing your arms; and
  - touching your face, nose, lips or hair.

- Use normal hand gestures but don't be manic – if you need to control your hands, clasp them in your lap.

- Concentrate on putting expression into your face.

- *Act* confident and you will *be* confident.

- Rehearse in front of a video camera to polish your performance.

Eye Contact

- Seek to establish rapport with your interviewer at the outset.

- Strive to maintain eye contact throughout.

- If eye contact disturbs you, focus on a point between their eyes.

- Always act as though the camera is on you – it might be! But avoid looking directly into the camera.

Your Voice

- Sit up straight, breathe deeply, and make your whole mouth work.

- Avoid speaking too quickly.

- Animate your voice.

- Avoid verbal ticks, like 'Well, er, um...'

- *Never* fake an accent.

- Use emphasis, but use it *wisely*.

- Practise on a cassette recorder – try reading stories out loud.

8 Putting your Point Across

Communicate

- Never let your material come between you and your audience.

- Seek to establish rapport.

- Don't memorise your material- the effect of conversation will be lost and you will sound stilted.

- Know your material and rehearse it – but aim for spontaneity.

Get Straight to the Point

- Don't bother with greetings or introductions.

- Time is always short so get to the point immediately.

- If you complete with time to spare reinforce your points – avoid introducing new ones.

Be Brief

- Strive for clarity and conciseness.

- Keep sentences short, simple and declarative.

- Avoid digging yourself into a hole.

- Leave out anything that would dilute your argument or distract from the main point.

- Keep each answer to 40 seconds or less, the length of a sound bite, to avoid repetition or qualification.

- Don't try to give an interview that's impossible to edit.

Be Positive

- Be positive about what you say and the way you say it.

- Aim to leave the interview on an upbeat.

- Be definite.

- Avoid sounding vague or equivocal.

End with Impact

- Your audience will base lasting impressions on the way you begin and end your interview. Your final statement should be:
  - strong;
  - emphatic;
  - positive; and
  - encouraging.

Live Interviews

- Live interviews are gone in a flash.

- Get your main point across right at the beginning – don't try to build up to it with a preamble.

- Be prepared to cut in in the last 30 seconds to get the rest of your message across, but:
  - first, check how long the interview is due to run;
  - hold your watch in your hand to keep track of the time; or
  - try to glimpse the floor manager's wind-up signal.

- Make your final point *quickly* – don't blunder on past the end of the interview.

Recorded Interviews

- Help the editor find your important points by flagging them, for example 'The critical thing is this...' etc.

- Don't say too much – the longer you talk, the more they'll cut out.

- If you make a mistake, stop... pause... recover... and make your point again. Then start the whole sentence again.

Give them an Inch...

- Say too much and your quotes may be telescoped, altering their meaning.

- Sensitive editing will improve your performance.

The Sound Bite

- The sound bite is the clip used to illustrate a report or news bulletin.

- It can range from seven seconds to 40 – 15 is about average.

- It may be short but it's worth it!

- Find out the average length of sound bite the programme uses – and tailor your message to fit.

- Make sure your message coincides with the one the reporter is looking for. For sound bites, reporters usually seek comment and reaction rather than a statement of the facts.

- Sound bites are often selected for dramatic impact.

- Rehearse it well but still sound spontaneous.

- Put it across with conviction.

- If they intend to take a range of bites, they will often follow the three interview stages:

  - your plans;
  - your answer to criticism of those plans;
  - and your next move.

- *Suggest* a 'What's Next' angle to keep your story bubbling.

- Offer to update the media.

- Be careful not to say too much – they might choose the wrong material!

9 Getting Out of a Tight Corner

- Most interviews are a straightforward exchange of information.

- Tricky approaches include:

  - The Adversarial interview. This consists of cross-examination to test every weakness. It is more common with politicians and pressure groups than business people, but *always* expect your argument to be tested; and stay cool if they attempt to shake your composure.

- The Buddy. Even sympathetic reporters are usually double-agents.
- The Barrister – Make sure the interviewer's summaries accurately reflect the story.
- The Manipulator – has a fixed idea about the story and will seek your endorsement for his interpretation.
- The Wise Monkey – asks questions selectively to reinforce his viewpoint or angle. Make sure he has the full picture.
- The Smiling Piranha – will lull you into a false sense of security to weaken your response to criticism.
- The Rumour-monger – will speculate to seek your confirmation or denial:
  * ask for the source of his information;
  * either give a *responsible* reason for prevaricating, but avoid giving a negative reply or repeating the rumour – or...
  * instead put over a point that is positive and active.

How to Handle your Interviewer

- The Golden Rule is DON'T LIE – the truth will out in the end and whatever you say *will* be used in evidence against you.

- Audience sympathy usually lies with the interviewer – to begin with.

  - If you're arrogant or abrasive towards him/her, you'll turn the audience against you.
  - Don't allow yourself to be walked over, but don't cosy up *too* much.
  - Stay cool, pleasant and positive – whatever the provocation – *never* lose your temper. Anger will be seen as unprofessional.

- It's the interviewer's job to test your argument by playing devil's advocate so:

  - expect it; and
  - *never* take it personally.

Killer Questions

- Anticipate killer questions.

233

- Counter the argument.
- Reassure the audience.
- Promote your viewpoint.

- Tilt the balance back in your favour – and do it in the first answer.

- The reporter may try to get you to establish a fact which he can use against you. Counter negative suggestions with positive assertions.

- Rehearse by taking the worse thing they could possibly ask you and combining it with the best thing you could possibly say – in one answer.

Correcting the Interviewer

- Pick up on major factual errors only.

- Correct them right away before they establish an impression.

- Do it good-naturedly.

- Don't be petty and pedantic.

- Avoid interrupting the interviewer unless he consistently gets his facts wrong.

- Don't let the interviewer interrupt you by:
  - adopting a determined tone;
  - raising your voice slightly;
  - fixing their eye; and
  - continuing until you've made your point.

Opinions

- Anticipate opposing points of view and prepare your counter arguments.

- Know what your opponents are saying

- Show that you understand their views and have found good, reliable grounds for thinking differently.

- It is better tactics to project your own position positively than to attack your opponent's.

- If your position is weak, a good interviewer will expose it.

- You must believe in your own position jf others are to believe In *you.*

Dealing with the Opposition

- If opponents' viewpoints will appear with yours in a recorded report ask for a transcript of what they're saying. This is not a right and you may be turned down. But if you succeed, you'll be able to tailor your comments to counter your opponents' arguments.

What if they don't ask the right questions?

- If the interview goes off on a tangent, turn it around and get your message across.

- Answer the question briefly then move on in the same sentence to make a positive point of your own before the interviewer can cut in.

- If the question is irrelevant then politely but firmly say so.

Squaring up to Trouble

- Recognise your danger zones.

- Anticipate difficult questions and prepare an answer for them.

- Plan a safe answer but make it as open and honest as possible.

- Don't stonewall. Be seen as human, caring and responsible, so if the interviewer pressed the point further he/she would seem irresponsible. The more the interviewer harasses *you*, the more audience sympathy will switch to you.

- Beware of questions you'd agreed not to discuss. Don't say 'We agreed not to talk about that!' Field it and go on to make a positive statement or find another opening to pick up on.
  - If it would *not* be damaging, acknowledge the point and move on to make one of your own.
  - If it *would* be damaging, refer immediately to another issue or precondition.

- If you need to put the interviewer in his place, attack the argument, not the interviewer himself.

- Be assertive, never aggressive.

- Use light humour to win audience sympathy.

- Always try to steer the interview back to your message – but never slavishly repeat prepared answers.

Don't go on the Defensive

- The audience will sense it and be convinced you have something to hide.
  Promote your positive arguments.

Beware the Pregnant Pause

- The pause trap is to keep you speaking and land yourself in it.

- Make your point and stop – or use the pause as an opportunity to go onto another point.

- Don't volunteer unhelpful information.

- You are not obliged to fill the pause gap, but the interviewer *is*.

Beware the Death Blow

- This is when the reporter decides to go for the jugular in the final moments.

236

- Don't offer a rebuttal- that would be negative.

- Cur in fast with a short, positive, statement to reinforce your message.

Troubleshooting Recorded Interviews

- In an emergency, you can pause it, interrupt it or stop it.

- For controversial interviews, have a colleague standing by to remind you of any points you missed and to step in discreetly if there's trouble.

- Interviews are usually sharper first take, so don't ask for repeats.

By the Way, That's Off the Record

- By the way, it might not be!

- Journalists are never off duty.

Doorstepping

This is where the media besiege you in the hope of a comment.

- Don't be forced into making an untimely statement.

- Never say 'no comment'

- Give a positive reason *why* you can't talk.

- Beam, be brisk and look confident

- Don't let your face give the game away

- Be polite

- Then keep moving!

It's a Cover up!

- NEVER he tempted to cover up or tell lies.

- Give honest answers and if you can't answer, give an honest reason why. If they've got you bang to rights, confess, be sorry, look to the future. In the end, it is seldom a matter of life and death where you are personally at risk.

- Treat media interviews as sport and set out to enjoy them.

10 Jubilation or Commiseration?

Cashing in on Fame

- Use your interview as a platform to reach other media outlets.

- Prepare in advance a news release around the message given in your interview. Insert a quote from the actual interview.

- Tailor it to national, local, trade or consumer press.

- Fax or courier it – then call to check they received it and to make yourself *available*.

- Send copies or transcripts of your interview to key clients or customers and for use in your internal press.

Learning from the Experience

- Study the recording and transcript to see how you could improve your performance.

- Get the criticism of a trusted colleague or consultant.

What if it Still *falls Apart?*

- Complaining *consumes* time and energy:
  - Is it worth it?
  - Could a reasonable phone call put matters right?

Broadcasting

- Your complaint might result in a correction but the damage will already be done.

- First register your complaint with the media.

- Get a transcript then complain up the line in stages from the producer to the company head to the regulatory bodies.

- Always complain to people by name.

The Press

- Guidelines are skimpier – so are corrections.

Libel

- If you think you might have been libelled take legal advice *immediately*. The tests are:
  - Was the statement wrong?
  - Is it likely to damage your reputation?

- Libel suits can be costly, even if you win.

- Train and prepare so you can acquit yourself more effectively in the future.

11 Training

A peak time news spot offers you millions of viewers, and can be worth more than one hundred thousand pounds in advertising. The stakes are too high to throw yourself on the media without training.

- Media training can be variable. Find out:
  - how much *practical* experience you will *personally* get; and
  - whether your tutor is speaking from experience.

- You should be given several cracks at being interviewed, with specific, personal feedback

- Choose training under the lights of a TV studio with multiple cameras to a visiting tutor with a single video. Several sessions will be necessary to improve upon your initial performance.

- You should be given the opportunity to work from authentic news releases – and see the end result as it would appear in the media.

- Consider a training session to put you through your paces before an appearance.

- Training session screentests can help companies select potential media performers. You can't tell how they'll come over until you see them on screen.

- With sensitive material and personal confidences at stake, select a training organisation you can trust. You will need to expose your weakness to them so they can strengthen your argument.

- To maintain and develop media skills, arrange top-up sessions at least once a year.

APPEND IX II:

USEFUL INFORMATION

Benn's Media Directory (Benn Business Information Services Ltd., PO Box 20, Sovereign Way, Tonbridge, Kent TN9 1RW. Tel: 0732 362666). International media information, including satellite and cable television.

British Rate and Data, (BRAD) (Maclean Hunter House, Chalk Lane, Cockfosters Road, Barnet, Herts EN4 OBU. Tel: 081 441 6644) Widely used source updated monthly to give details of national and regional newspapers, TV and radio, new launches and demises.

Editors (PR Newslink, 9-10, Great Sutton Street, London ECI V OBX. Tel: 071 251 9000). Six volume listing of newspapers, magazines, radio TV and trade press, naming individual correspondents. The Mediadisk service, also offers PR planning on a computer disk.

Hollis Press and Public Relations Annual (Contact House, Lower Hampton Road, Sunbury-on-Thames MDX TW16 5HG. Tel: 0932784781) PR consultancies in the UK and Abroad.

Pims Media Directory (PIMS, 4, St. John's Place, London EC1M 4AH. Tel: 071 250 0870). Lists contacts in the trade and technical press as well as national and regional newspapers, broadcasting and news agencies. It also gives contacts for consumer-related items and publishes a European edition.

The Blue Book of British Broadcasting, (Tellex Monitors, Communications House, 210 Old Street, London, ECIV 9UN Tel: 071 490 8018). Comprehensive guide to the key contacts in radio and television in the UK, with details of programme schedules.

The Writers' and Artists' Yearbook, (A&C Black, London – available bookshops) lists newspapers and magazines by country and classification and offers a list of freelance agencies. Generalist rather than specialist.

The Writers' Handbook, (MacMillan – available bookshops). Also gives general details of national and regional newspapers and magazines, extending to television and radio.

Willings Press Guide, (Thomas Skinner Directories, Windsor Court, East Grinstead House, East Grinstead, West Sussex, RH19 1XA Tel: 0342 326972). Two volume professional guide to newspapers and periodicals in the UK and 125 other countries. It offers a nation by nation alphabetical list, a classified index for niche targeting and a UK index of town and counties for local targeting. It reports ceased publications, which makes it easer to update your own media list, and includes readership profiles.

Transcript Services

Transcripts of current television and radio broadcasts are obtainable commercially from:

Tellex Monitors, Communications House, 210 Old Street, London ECIV 9UN. Tel: 071 4908018. Short transcripts can be faxed within 20 minutes.

The Broadcast Monitoring Company, Register House, 4 Holford Yard, Cruikshanks Street, London WCIX 9HD. Tel. 071 833 1055.

Complaints

The Director General, BBC, Broadcasting House, Portland Place, London WIA 1AA. Tel: 071 5804468.

The Secretary, Broadcasting Complaints Commission, Grosvenor Gardens House, 35-7 Grosvenor Gardens, London SW1W OBS. Tel: 071 630 1966.

Independent Television Commission, 70 Brompton Road, London SW3 1 EY. Tel: 071 584 7011.

The Director, The Press Complaints Commission, 1 Salisbury Square, London, EC4Y 8AE. Tel: 071 353 1248.

The Radio Authority, 70 Brompton Road, London SW3 lEY. Tel: 071581 2888.

Recommended Reading:

Be Your Own PR Man: A Public Relations Guide for the Small Businessman, Michael Bland, Kogan Page, 1981.
Broadcast Journalism, Andrew Boyd, Heinemann, 1988.
Getting Publicity, David Morgan Rees, David and Charles, 1984.
How to Get Your Point Across in 30 Seconds or Less, Milo O. Frank, Corgi, 1987.
How To Take On The Media, Sarah Dickinson, Weidenfeld and Nicholson, London, 1990.
Promoting Yourself on Television and Radio, Michael Bland and Simone Mondesir, Kogan Page, 1987.
Successful Media Relations, Judith Ridgeway, Gower, 1984. *Surviving the Media Jungle,* Dina Ross, Mercury, 1990.
The Activist's Handbook, Making More than Futile Gestures, Bob Houlton, Arrow Books, 1975.
The headline business, a businessman's guide to working with the media, compiled by Squire Barraclough, CBI in association with Abbey Life Assurance Co. Ltd, 1981 (Available from the CBI, Centre Point, 103, New Oxford Street, London WCIA 1DU).
TV & Radio – Everybody's Soapbox, Bruce Parker and Nigel Farrell, Blandford Press 1983.
Using the Media, Denis MacShane, Pluto Press, 1979.

REFERENCES

1 How to Grab Them By the Ears

1. *Be Your Own PR Man*, Kogan Page, 1981 p.14.
2. *Broadcast Journalism*, Andrew Boyd, Heinemann, 1988.
3. Dina Ross, Mercury, 1990.
4. *UK Press Gazette*, 3.7.89.
5. Table 7.5, HMSO, 1988.
6. Channel 4, 5.11.89.
7. *How to take on the media*, Weidenfeld Paperbacks, 1990.
8. ibid. 3.
9. Introduction to 'Contact', IPC Media Publications, 1980-81.
10. 18.5.89.

2 Should You Give the Interview?

1. Thorn in the Labour Rose', George Hill, *The Times*, 31.5.89.
2. Shell UK figure, 1991.
3. *Surviving The Media Jungle*, Dina Ross, Mercury, 1990 p.5.
4. BBC 1989.
5. February 1991.
6. *Getting Publicity*, David and Charles, 1984.
7. 21.7.90.

3 Preparing the Interview

1. *The Media Show*, Channel 4, 5.11.89.
2. *How To Get Your Point Across In 30 Seconds Or Less*, Milo O. Frank, Corgi, 1986, p.39.

3. 1981, compiled by Squire Barraclough.
4. CBI, Abbey Life Assurance, 1981.
5. Quoted in *Broadcast journalism*, Andrew Boyd, Heinemann, 19: developed from *Language in Thought and Action*, Harcourt, Brace and World, 1964.
6. Mercury, 1990, p.153.

4 The Television Interview

1. Parker and Farrell, Blandford Press, 1983.
2. *The headline business*, CBI, Abbey Life, 1981.
3. *Daily Telegraph*, 14.8.84.
4. *The Times*, 31.5.89.
5. Pluto, 1979, p.139.
6. 24.2.91.

5 The Radio Interview

1. *Radio*, March 1989.
2. From, *Broadcast journalism*, Andrew Boyd, Heinemann, 1988.
3. 19.5.91.

6 Newspaper and Magazine Interviews

1. How DOES Lynn Barber Do It?', 24.2.91, drawn from *Mostly Men*, Viking 1991.
2. 'Convert on the Long Trek', interview with F.W. de Klerk, 28.4.91
3. 'Caught In The Camera, The Leader As Subject', 25.11.90.
4. 'Saying the Unsayable about the Germans', Dominic Lawson, *The Spectator*, 14.7.90.
5. Diary, *The Spectator*, 21.7.90.

7 Putting Yourself Across

1. 'Beware head-butt, doggy-wag and hammer nod', Hugh Hebert, *The Guardian*, 16.10.89.
2. 'Alias Smith and Brown,' 7.10.90.
3. *How to Get Your Point Across in 30 Seconds or Less*, Corgi 1987.
4. 'Caught in the Camera, The Leader as Subject', Sally Soames, *The Sunday Times*, 25.11.90.
5. Bland and Mondesir, Kogan Page, 1987, p.130.
6. From *Broadcast Journalism*, Andrew Boyd, Heinemann, 1988

8 Putting Your Point Across

1. Derek Morgan, *The Times*, 31.5.89.
2. 'How to go on air and survive,' *The Times*, 31.5.89.
3. From BIM Management Review and Digest, Vol. 5 No.1, reprinted in *The headline business*, CBI/Abbey Life 1981.
4. Ibid. 2.
5. *'Gift of the Gab'*, BBC2, August 1989.
6. 'Illumination over Sunday Lunch', Gillian Reynolds, *Daily Telegraph*, 3.12.90.
7. Pluto Press, 1979, p.151.
8. Milo O. Frank, Corgi, 1986, pp.16-17.
9. *The Media Show*, Channel 4, 5.11.89.
10. 'Image makers come to the aid of the party', Robin Hunt, *Sunday Correspondent*, 8.10.90.

9 Getting Out of a Tight Corner

1. 'Who's been Paxmanned?' 11-17 August 1990.
2. 'BBC interviewers need to be sharper', Maggie Brown, *The Independent*, 27.7.90.
3. 'The Radio Show even Thatcher wouldn't miss', Cathy Galvin, *Daily Express*, 18.3.89.
4. Weidenfeld Paperbacks, 1990.
5. Gower 1984.
6. *Getting Publicity*, David and Charles, 1984, pA2.

7. 'How DOES Lynn Barber Do It?', 24.2.91, drawn from *Mostly Men*, Lynn Barber, Viking 1991.

8. Pluto Press, 1979.

9. Kogan Page, 1987.

10. Extracted from 'The Talk-masters of television', Peter Freedman, *The Independent*, 7.6.89.

11. *The Independent*, 17.5.89.

12. UK Press Gazette, Opinion, 28.5.90.

13. 13.11.89.

14. Ibid 13.

15. 'Bunfight At The KO Corral', 19.7.89.

16. Mercury, 1990, p.169.

17. 1989, p.76.

18. From *The headline business*, CBI/Abbey Life, 1981, p.l5.

19. BBC Radio 4, 14.6.91.

20. *Media Show*, Channel 4, 29.1.89.

21. *Radio*, March 1989.

INDEX